THE FINE ARTIST'S GUIDE TO SHOWING AND SELLING YOUR WORK

ACKNOWLEDGMENTS

I gratefully acknowledge the willingness of the fine artists included in this book to share their business materials, expertise and insight. Without their input, this book could not have been completed. I also thank editor Susan Conner for her patient guidance and art director Carol Buchanan for her expert assistance.

ABOUT THE AUTHOR

Sally Prince Davis is an art marketing consultant, freelance writer, and speaker on the business of art at art workshops and conferences across the country. She is also the author of *The Graphic Artist's Guide to Marketing and Self-Promotion*. She is the former "Strictly Business" columnist for *The Artist's Magazine* and former editor of the annual directory, *Artist's Market*.

THE FINE ARTIST'S GUIDE TO
SHOWING AND SELLING YOUR WORK

Sally Prince Davis

NORTH LIGHT BOOKS Cincinnati, Ohio

The Fine Artist's Guide to Showing and Selling Your Work. Published by North Light Books, an imprint of F&W Publications, 1507 Dana Avenue, Cincinnati, Ohio 45207.

Manufactured in the United States.

93 92 91 90 89   5 4 3 2 1

Library of Congress Cataloging-in-Publication Data

Davis, Sally Prince
   The fine artist's guide to showing and selling your work/Sally Prince Davis.
     p.   cm.
   Bibliography: p.
   Includes index.
   ISBN 0-89134-308-3
     1. Art—Vocational guidance—United States. 2. Art—Marketing—United States. I. Title.
   N6505.D36   1989   89-3224
   706'.8'8—dc19   CIP

Editor: Susan Conner
Designer: Carol Buchanan

This book is dedicated to
Ruth and Donald Prince
and
Eleanora and Charles Davis

CONTENTS

INTRODUCTION

The world of fine art is in a cautiously wonderful position. As more and more artists seek to express themselves creatively, there is an abundance of excellent work. This means, overall, the average person is more exposed to fine art and accepts it as an integral part of the living/working environment. Translation? Sales.

The fine artist, however, must deal with an art field tight with increased competition. To have your work sell, you must make people aware of it, tell them where they can see it, and how it can be purchased. In other words, you must be your own marketing and promotion director as well as an artist. Now, more than ever, it's a necessity to combine art and business skills to have a financially successful fine art career, whether your sales are full time, part time or occasional.

In talking with artists, I learned that the areas of marketing and self-promotion remain a mystery to many of you. Some of you have been marketing your work for a while, however haphazardly and sporadically; you must concentrate your efforts on a specific marketing program. Others of you are experienced artists, but newcomers to marketing: you feel lost and are looking for specific steps to take to begin this new journey. Then there are those of you who are absolutely terrified of marketing; you haven't tried it and don't even want to think about it. However, you want to sell your work. These two seemingly opposite feelings (which aren't uncommon) come together if you learn to view your marketing efforts as an opportunity to be your most creative self. You will discover that marketing and self-promotion are merely different aspects of your artistic self-expression.

In this book, I chose to focus specifically on marketing and self-promotion in order to address the issues that plague many of you. By concentrating on these two areas, I can best help you to understand exactly what marketing and self-promotion entail. I also discuss the specific market areas that exist for you, how to determine where you and your work fit, how to evaluate and what to expect of the various types of outlets, and how to create a marketing/self-promotion program that will give you the greatest advantage for sales. This book will demystify marketing for all artists and provide guideposts to make the trip toward sales easier.

Use the information in this book as a base upon which to build success in showing and selling your work. You know best where you stand and how close you are to your goals. Read and adapt the basics emphasized here to your own situation and goals. Then believe in your work and in yourself. Approach marketing and self-promotion with rightful confidence, and watch as your lifelong dream of showing and selling your work blossoms.

—Sally Prince Davis

CHAPTER 1
ART IS BUSINESS

You, as an artist, invest time, money, emotions, skill, and talent in your work. You evaluate these factors and set monetary prices to your paintings. You know that, besides being financially rewarding, having your work purchased is a form of praise—someone agrees with you regarding the painting's value and wants to include your artwork in his environment.

But between pricing your artwork and actually receiving the income and praise, you are confronted with a whole new world—business. And the business world, at first glance, might appear to be the antithesis of all you've known in your world of art.

Not true. Business and art team up to enhance your art career and enable you to reach your creative potential. Just as you developed your artistic talent, you can develop skills, habits, and knowledge that help you appreciate the challenge and creativity involved in marketing and self-promotion. You'll quickly learn the value of being a good businessperson: your art is seen, appreciated, and purchased; your reputation as a creative person is enhanced; and you become more financially secure, giving you more time to devote to your art. Self-satisfaction and confidence grow as the public pays your work the respect it's due.

Every product and service you use has been marketed to you in some way—through print advertisements, TV commercials, mailed flyers, or a personal sales contact. For a product to sell, its manufacturer must do three things: let you, the consumer, know it exists; explain how it meets your desires; and describe how and where you can buy it.

These are exactly the same steps to follow with *your* product—your talent and artwork—to realize its sale. By doing research, establishing a marketing plan, and creating the right marketing tools, you'll reach the appropriate outlets and buyers for your work.

MAKING A BUSINESS COMMITMENT

Your primary commitment is to art, either on a full-time, part-time, or hobby basis; you must also make a serious commitment to business.

Your business commitment should contain the same degree of dedication and promise as your commitment to art. You must be willing to set aside specific amounts of time, money, and effort devoted only to business in order to have your artwork seen, appreciated, respected, and purchased.

For every hour devoted to painting, set aside an hour for business. Unrealistic? No, because "business" includes stops at the art store, phone calls to a gallery, research trips to new outlets, days spent at booth shows, and trips to the printer for new business cards. Business hours don't have to equal painting hours on a daily basis, but you should pay some attention to business every day.

As well as allotting time for business, you must set aside money to support your business efforts. It's impossible to state an exact monetary figure because the amount is very artist-specific. Variables encountered are:

■ Prior marketing efforts. You need less money if you're building on a base of previously developed business materials rather than starting from scratch.

■ Scope of marketing—local or national. Mailed submissions for national marketing require money for envelopes and postage in addition to samples and printed materials.

■ Market area you're considering. Very sophisticated galleries demand professionally designed and printed marketing pieces; you might need to hire a designer.

■ Your photographic skills. To obtain the best samples, you might need to hire a photographer.

In order to determine what's necessary for you to accomplish a successful ongoing marketing and promotional campaign, you must estimate your costs. If you have a consistent income, either from art, another job, a spouse, or a friend, calculate the percentage of that income that can be set aside monthly as a base

DEALING WITH BUSINESS

Cincinnati, Ohio, painter Valerie Shesko admits that she dislikes the business side of art, but also knows that, in order to sell art, business responsibilities are inevitable. Judicious planning and the establishment of good business habits allow her to keep her priorities in order. "I realize that what's important for me is to keep my time freed up when I'm creatively 'hot.' There are times when your work is going really well and other times when it's slow. If you can be organized enough so that you can continue to send out work or make connections without coming to a complete stop in the studio, that's ideal. I don't want to come to a complete stop creatively to do whatever it is I'm supposed to do for business."

Shesko believes that business aspects needn't impinge upon creativity as long as you understand the importance of controlling your time. "If you're in control, you can get more of the time you *want* for your creative work. And if you don't watch out for your best creative time, then it's going to be eaten up by other things."

And she has experienced firsthand how events can get out of hand. "For example, I knew I was going to have to ship paintings to New York because they were going to a show in Germany. But the show organizers could only tell me that the shipping date was some time in the fall. When they finally called with the final date, I had only about a week's notice to get those paintings to New York. I looked at my calendar and realized I was really counting on working full-time in my studio that week, not spending days getting lumber, building crates, and calling around to get the best price on shipping."

Shesko decided her priority was creativity—"I was on a roll!"—and that she couldn't give up the days painting in her studio. She opted for a transportation service that would handle all services for her from crating to shipping. It cost twice as much, but "I finished a painting in those three studio days, so it was well worth what I had to spend for shipping."

Experience also helps Shesko to balance business and art. She backed off of full-time promotion while she returned to school to receive her MFA in painting, and pulled her work out of all of the galleries representing her except one because she couldn't keep them supplied. She continued to pick up her solo shows and the regular exhibition schedule that she had previously kept.

"National competitive shows are the thrust of my self-promotion right now and I know when they're coming. I know there's a bunch of them in early fall, then there's a lull, then another bunch around March. Knowing all this helps. When you've done the rounds a couple of times, you know what to expect and you start to mentally save your work and to keep up with your photography. This way you're not caught in a crunch—you don't suddenly have to stop and take your work to a photographer." She suggests getting slides done regularly so they're in your studio and labeled. Then you don't have to stop everything if an unexpected opportunity suddenly pops up.

Claiming that she's learned a great deal the hard way, Shesko passes along other tips that help her to stay in control, not only of her time, but also of her business.

Tip 1. "I inherited a small computer which I use for writing letters, but most of all use for my record-keeping. There's a program called Checks and Balances (available from CDE Software) that's ideal for artists like me whose business requires more than tallying receipts at the end of the year, but isn't so complicated that it needs a spreadsheet program. This program is a great intermediary step, and it's very user friendly. When it comes up on the computer screen, it looks just like a checkbook. You simply put in the number of the check you wrote, the amount, and to whom it was written. You key it to the appropriate category, such as supplies, depreciation, utilities, etc., and the program automatically deducts or adds the amount. At any time, I can type in a category, like supplies, and the computer prints out the whole list of all the checks written for supplies by check number, amount, and to whom paid. At the end of the year, all I do is print out a list for each category and hand it over to my accountant with my receipts."

Tip 2. "I keep an open hanging file for all of my receipts and slips right by the door where I walk in. I've found this to be the most convenient place even though it's not in my actual business area because it's where I can see it. It makes it easy for me to walk in the door and immediately file my receipts. This portable file is a box with hanging files in it, and I've labeled each file to correspond to the categories I use with my Checks and Balances computer program. In turn, these categories are the ones that correspond to Schedule C, the IRS tax form that my accountant uses. I used to have a lot of separate categories, only to find that my accountant lumped them all together to correspond to Schedule C anyway."

Tip 3. "I have my artwork photographed and duplicated professionally. When the slides come back to me, the originals and duplicates are indistinguishable because all are mounted in plain white cardboard mounts. In order to tell them apart, I put a different color marker on the very top edge of the slide mount where it's very unobtrusive. But I can tell at a glance, then, that if it's black on the top, it's an original; if it's green, it's a duplicate. Other artists might want to do this for different media so they can tell at a glance, without even looking at the slide's image, whether it's a work on paper, a painting on canvas, or a sculpture."

Tip 4. "Whenever I make a long-distance phone call, I jot down the phone number, time, and purpose of the call while the phone is ringing. I throw these notes into my file. Then at the end of the year, I can take out our phone bills and circle the ones that are my business calls."

Tip 5. "I save artists' invitations that I receive when there's something interesting about them. I keep them on file to remind me of alternatives I otherwise might not think of when I have to design my own invitation. It might just be a little thing, like the kind of lettering or the diagonal layout, but it keeps me fresh."

Tip 6. "When I go to a gallery, especially if I'm visiting out of town, and I see an artist's work I admire or whose work is similar to mine, I ask for his or her resume and make note of the *other* galleries that artist is in. For example, the artist might live in Massachusetts, but have work in galleries in Texas and New Mexico. Right now I might not be looking for a gallery in those states, but when I do I may hit those galleries first because I know that they're open to work like mine. I've always found that an artist's resume can teach you a lot; for example, where they've had shows can be very useful to you."

of ready cash for marketing expenses. If your income fluctuates, anticipate your financial needs for marketing so money can be banked during "fat" months to cover the "lean" ones. By using a marketing calendar, discussed in Chapter 5, you can pinpoint when marketing money will be needed.

Perhaps at this point you can't determine exactly how much money you'll need, but here are some guidelines:

■ Spend the most money on your samples. These are reproductions (slides or photographs) made from your actual original works. These samples are your "salespeople," the examples that are going to sell your work when the reviewer/buyer can't see the original; therefore, they must be absolutely the best. Allocate as much money as possible to obtain professional photography and quality color lab work.

■ Start with the basic marketing/promotional tools—business cards, letterhead, envelopes. Don't cut corners with shoddy printing or low-quality paper. It's better to have only these very basic materials printed very well on good quality paper than to have an extensive marketing package that looks amateurish and cheap. This is a time when quality outweighs quantity.

■ If you already have basic marketing tools that you like and that accurately reflect you and your work as they are today, build on these materials. Design every other piece so that it coordinates with these basic materials and presents a unified visual package. Select the same paper color (if reasonable), type style, or one unifying graphic element, such as a repeated logo, to pull diverse pieces together. Keep in mind that colored printing and paper is more expensive than black printing on white paper.

■ Talk with your printer. As you begin to develop brochures and mailers, listen to what the printer says can and can't be done with your design. Be candid about the amount of money you can spend. Often a printer can develop very creative ways to print your pieces, once your goals and finances are understood. Sometimes it's by printing four mailers at once because it's cheaper to print "four up"; some-

times printers get unexpected buys on paper and you benefit from their savings.

OFFICE SPACE

As a serious, self-employed businessperson, establish an area conducive to the affairs of business. Your studio is equipped for creating art, but is it prepared for conducting business? The materials involved in marketing, self-promotion, and record-keeping must be as organized and available as your art materials.

To promote a business environment, you need a desk (or large flat table), file cabinet, bookcase, storage rack or area, and a good desk lamp. The desk or table is off-limits to art materials; this area is designated "for business only"—a space where you can work on business matters freely and avoid procrastination. A clear, clean desk is harder to avoid—it keeps calling to you.

The file cabinet is for organizing business articles, tax forms, business licenses, and receipts. If a metal file cabinet is too expensive, consider purchasing cardboard containers with hanging file racks. Scan your local paper for used office equipment; metal file cabinets can be purchased for a fraction of their original cost.

A bookcase is needed as your collection of business-related books, magazines, booklets and pamphlets increases.

A storage rack or area organizes your marketing and self-promotional tools as they're developed. It's the place to keep your slides or photographs dry and out of the sun, your brochures cataloged, mailers arranged according to date (so you're never sending out-dated materials), and the original paste-ups that created these materials.

A good desk lamp is self-explanatory. Your business-related activities are more easily accomplished if you can clearly see what you're doing.

All business furnishings can be incorporated into your actual studio space, but if it isn't large enough, set up a business area nearby that is yours when you need it. Office furnishings often can be placed in living areas without disruption.

Two other pieces of equipment to consider for your office are a home computer and a personal copier. These two pieces of equipment are expensive but, depending on the extent of your art business, may be worthwhile in the long run. A home computer can organize mailing lists and inventory, as well as track expenses and income. A photocopier duplicates cover letters, resumes, invoices, contracts and letters of agreement, and reply cards.

The Importance of Privacy

Art is your business product. You must be able to produce it on a consistent basis with a minimum of outside interference. Private space is an absolute necessity for you to take yourself and your art career seriously.

Ideally, if you live in a single-family home with other family members, your office/studio is in a building separate from the main household, such as a converted garage. If this isn't possible, work with other family members to convert a bedroom or den into a studio. Not only does this give you the room you need to be your most creative, but it impresses upon others how dedicated you are to your art.

If you live in a small apartment or loft where it's impossible to have a room to yourself, build or buy inexpensive screens to set up, or hang divider curtains from the ceiling. If you can't use either of these suggestions, give serious thought to what you *can* do to cut yourself off visually from the rest of the living areas. Art is now your business and you need a protected environment in which to grow and produce.

Family and friends, well-meaning as they are, have a way of invading privacy, usually at the least-welcomed moments. Because many artists work from their homes, their work is taken less seriously by others (indeed, many times it isn't perceived as work at all). Interruptions are constant—errands to be run, baby-sitting, golf games, dinner plans, yard work, and so on.

What do you do? First and foremost, set aside a regular number of hours when you will be at work, that is, either painting or handling business matters. These can be regular business hours, such as 9 to 5, or, for part-time artists, perhaps 10 to 2 in the day or 8 to 10 in the evening.

During these specific hours, go into your private area and *work*—family members need to know that you are not to be disturbed. A phone answering machine prevents disturbing phone calls; a speaker device allows you to monitor calls and respond to an emergency. Arrange day care or baby-sitting for very young children if their care is cutting significantly into your work hours. Schedule errand-running and outings around your work hours just as you would if you were working at an outside job.

Once family members and friends see how serious you are about making a success of your art, you'll detect a subtle difference in their thinking. On the other hand, if you constantly place your art and its related business activities in second place, your career will be second-rate, at least in the minds of family and friends. Allow it to be equally as important as an outside occupation.

In conducting a business you lose some privacy simply because your phone number and address are on your business materials, which are widely distributed. If this is a real concern to you, consider renting a post office box which allows mail deliveries without disclosure of your home address. This is also wise if you anticipate moving several times within the same city—business materials remain accurate without constant reprinting.

Running a Business from Your Home

A home-based business allows flexibility, saves time (no commuting), and represents a degree of self-determination and freedom, but it also comes with unique, inherent problems, such as:

■ *Isolation.* You may be accustomed to painting alone, but now you're also a self-employed businessperson running a business alone. You can experience a feeling of isolation. There's no one around to make business decisions for you, to tell you where to market, how to best communicate your artwork to potential buyers, when to do a mailing, how to handle the nagging paperwork, or to help untangle business problems.

Yes, you are alone, but the positive side is that your business is entirely yours. You are *creating* in business just as you create in painting. If someone else were telling you what decisions to make, it would be his art career, not yours. No one makes the wisest decision every time, but the self-employed person receives the rewards for the good decisions and learns from the not-so-good ones.

Business knowledge builds on itself. Establish a strong base for informed decisions by reading business books, attending business workshops for the small businessperson, joining national and local associations, especially those that emphasize business information for artists, and by reading artists' magazines. Apply the self-discipline of routine to handling daily paperwork and know that outside professionals—accountants, tax specialists, attorneys—can be called to resolve business situations that aren't routine.

■ *Temptation.* Whether in the form of the refrigerator or television set, a racquetball game or dirty dishes, temptation rears its head and tries to keep you from working. Entire workdays disappear unless you discipline yourself to stick to regular work hours. Taking "a minute" to fold the laundry, finish that magazine article, or check the car's oil can actually steal an hour away from your business day.

■ *Makeshift Environment.* Home is home and business is business until you plan to meet business clients at home. These clients might be a young couple wanting to commission you to do a portrait of their daughter, or high-powered interior decorators interested in numerous pieces of your work for a new office building. Either way, you need to create as much of a businesslike atmosphere as possible.

If you anticipate frequent client visits, prepare a separate room, possibly adjoining your studio, where there is comfortable seating, a door that can be closed, and soundproofing. Inform family members that no interruptions are allowed while you're meeting a client.

If this ideal situation can't be met, arrange for another room in the home in which client meetings can occur without disruption. It might mean sending family members to a movie or arranging baby-sitting at someone else's home for small children. To create an appropriate business discussion atmosphere,

you do not want a television on in the same room, teenagers raiding the refrigerator, small children playing underfoot, or a spouse interjecting opinions. All of these distract from the business at hand—your artwork.

■ *Clients' Attitudes.* Some clients, because they are coming to your home, think that you will charge less for your work because you don't have a "real" studio. Counteract this attitude by dressing in a businesslike manner, being prepared with all the materials necessary for the meeting, and presenting a comfortable space free from distractions. You will immediately convey that you are a serious, professional artist who deals fairly yet demands respect.

DEALING WITH REJECTION— AND SUCCESS

One of the hazards of selling your artwork is that you're wide open for criticism—and rejection. It's no fun, but everyone, no matter how famous, has had to deal with both.

A gallery director tells you your work doesn't fit the gallery, though you believe it does. A competition returns your slides. A booth show you've been in before turns you down. The reasons vary, but they add up to the reality that rejection is a part of business. It's still hard to deal with, though, especially if there are several rejections in a row, and it can be depressing.

To help understand rejection, you must accept several facts about business.

Reality Number 1. Your creativity, once you begin to market your work, is a business product. No matter how much of yourself is in your artwork, no matter the skill and the talent, if your work isn't marketable for the outlet you're approaching at the time you approach it, your work's going to be turned down.

Reality Number 2. Your artwork is not going to please all people all of the time—and it shouldn't. The importance of a firm faith in yourself and your work can't be overstated. Balance this inner faith with rational thought—identify critical points in any negative response to your work and weigh their validity—sometimes negativity can be a turning point for growth. Negativity hurts; feel the hurt, but move beyond it. Learn from constructive advice, and go on.

Reality Number 3. There will not be *one* gallery, *one* award, or *one* show that's going to "make it" for you. Your career will be a series of sales, awards, commissions, and exhibitions, each adding and complementing the other. Your financial status presumably will increase as your reputation grows, but your career will carry on in a continuum, not a windfall. As one success comes your way, lay the groundwork through marketing and self-promotion to ensure another.

If rejection does get a stranglehold on you, there are some things you can do to break its hold.

First, keep it in perspective. Rejection is only one person's opinion of your work, and that person is viewing it with individual preferences and art needs in mind. Luck and timing play nearly as important a role in selling your work as do talent and skill. Your work was simply in the wrong place at the wrong time.

Second, cultivate a support system—other artists, family, or friends to whom you can turn for empathy and/or advice. Select people to whom you can pour out your anger, knowing that your words will go no further. A person who can reinforce the positive aspects of you and your talent is a bonus.

If no such friends and family exist for you right now, be your own self-esteem booster by focusing on the uniqueness and good within your work and the past successes you've had. Invent a ritual that leads to good and worthwhile feelings. Pamper yourself with a mood lifter. It's different for each of us: reading quietly for an hour, shopping, cooking, tinkering with the car, pursuing a non-art-related hobby, daydreaming, listening to music.

Third, don't take rejection personally. Feeling rebuffed and unappreciated generates anger. Suppressed anger can lead to dejection, serious depression, a drop in self-confidence, and artist's block. Don't keep anger inside! Vent it to that trusted friend, if possible. If not, remember that anger is energy—burn up the energy and dissipate the anger through exer-

cise. Punch a pillow, jog, do aerobics, walk, swim, run in place—any activity that burns up negative energy and leaves your spirit balanced and ready for positive input.

Fourth, lessen the possibility of future rejections. Research markets thoroughly, approach outlets most appropriate for your work, and evaluate your business materials. Do they communicate your value? Do they need updating? Is it time to investigate new market areas?

Success, strange as it seems, also has pitfalls. For the sake of simplicity, success is defined here in monetary terms.

When your works begin to command high prices, the sudden influx of money can create pressures you didn't have when you were a relative unknown. Money management is crucial; promote future security by saving or investing part of that money. The art world is fickle, and your works may not always command high prices.

Another pitfall of success is that, as works bring in higher and higher prices, some artists feel the pressure of living up to their reputations. Each new painting must somehow be "worthy" of the high fees or must be what the public expects to see. Artists in this position find themselves trapped between topping their last painting and wanting—needing—to grow creatively. Some react by overindulging in drugs or alcohol or by suffering artist's block.

Excessive indulgence in either drugs or alcohol is not the answer. They dull your creative edge and steal valuable artistic time. Overcome temporary artist's block by relaxing with a pen or pencil in your hand, by leaving the project and returning to it at a later time, or by determining the reason for the block—perhaps fear of failure, fatigue, or worry over an extraneous problem.

In summary, to keep rejection from overwhelming you, keep it in perspective, cultivate a support system, invent a ritual that makes you feel good and worthwhile, burn up negative energy and replace it with positive feelings, and lessen the possibility of future rejections through solid marketing research.

CHAPTER ONE
CHECKLISTS

Use your marketing funds wisely by:
☐ Spending most on artwork samples, usually slides or photographs
☐ Starting with basic marketing and promotional tools
☐ Building on basic materials by matching paper, color, and type-style—remember that black ink and white paper are cheaper than color
☐ Getting more than one price quote for printing, preferably three
☐ Discussing your marketing tools with a reliable printer and
☐ Exploring quantity printing and possible paper buys

The minimum equipment you'll need for your business space:
☐ A desk or large flat table
☐ File cabinet, file holders, and labels
☐ Bookcase
☐ Storage rack or area
☐ Good desk lamp
☐ Index card box
☐ Record-keeping book
☐ Accordion files or pocket folders

Optional equipment you can consider buying:
☐ Personal computer
☐ Photocopier
☐ Separate business telephone
☐ Phone answering machine
☐ Bulletin board
☐ Post office box

To work successfully from a home-based studio:
☐ Create a private work area
☐ Establish regular work hours
☐ Set specific times for coffee and meal breaks
☐ Arrange for child care if necessary
☐ Schedule errands around work hours
☐ Develop a business attitude
☐ Consult outside business professionals to help resolve complex problems
☐ Create a business environment in your studio or office
☐ Exercise regularly and eat well-balanced meals
☐ Develop interests outside your art

To work from a home-based studio, don't:
☐ Steal time from your work hours
☐ Allow family and friends to interrupt your work with nonemergency problems
☐ Overeat
☐ Indulge in alcohol or drugs
☐ Forget about your appearance
☐ Think less of your business because it's at home
☐ Hesitate to ask for the respect and money due you
☐ Allow children to interfere with business meetings
☐ Let your art consume family time

To build your knowledge of business:
- ☐ Read books and magazines on business management
- ☐ Attend workshops geared to the small-business person
- ☐ Join national and local business organizations
- ☐ Talk with outside business professionals
- ☐ Contact the Small Business Administration office in your area
- ☐ Take entrepreneurship classes at a local college or trade school
- ☐ Network with other artists

To deal with rejection:
- ☐ Keep it in perspective
- ☐ Realize your art is a business product, not suited to everyone's taste
- ☐ Understand that some rejection is inevitable
- ☐ Cultivate a support system
- ☐ Invent a ritual that makes you feel good and worthwhile
- ☐ Don't allow anger over rejection to become suppressed
- ☐ Lessen the possibility of future rejection through better market research
- ☐ Contact a mental health professional if suffering severe depression

To deal with success:
- ☐ Investigate money management so you will reap further rewards
- ☐ Be aware of pressure to live up to your fame
- ☐ Budget time to keep up with increased production schedule

CHAPTER 2
FINE ART MARKETS

Before any actual marketing endeavors begin, you need to understand the fine art markets available to you. Fine art careers often call for marketing in more than one area, so it's important to learn about all of the fine art markets. This gives you a broad base of knowledge from which to work when it is time to select your primary areas of interest for your marketing.

The advantages, disadvantages, and general business practices of five of the most common market areas—galleries, shops, booth shows, competitions, and commissions—are discussed here, followed by a look at some alternative markets and three graphic art markets frequently open to fine art.

RETAIL GALLERIES

Retail galleries are in business to sell artists' works. They appear in all shapes and sizes, from very formal, viewing-by-appointment-only salons, to very relaxed, come-in-your-jeans-and-see-what-we-have mall galleries. Some restrict themselves to a specific price range, style, or subject matter; others welcome any type of artwork. Some galleries specialize in emerging artists; others handle only established artists with solid reputations. Your work fits into one or more of these galleries; the hard part is finding which ones are right for you.

Many artists can and do sell their work without being represented in a gallery. But galleries do have their advantages.

■ The greatest advantage is that someone else handles your art sales. Once a work is in a gallery, the artist doesn't have to "sell" to a potential buyer, complete the paperwork, worry that a check will bounce, collect the sales tax, or deal with shipping. Gallery sales personnel carry out these details.

■ More potential buyers see your work in a gallery. As retail businesses in shopping areas, galleries are much more likely to attract potential buyers than is an artist's solitary studio.

■ A gallery's reputation can enhance your own, since many buyers return to a gallery they know and trust. For example, if a gallery has the reputation of showing artists whose works routinely increase in value, having your work here can hand your career a sound boost. Also, it affirms that your work is considered salable by someone whose business is the sale of art.

Galleries have their disadvantages, also. The greatest one is the flip side to their greatest advantage; that is, you, the creator of the work, *don't* get the opportunity to meet its buyers and discuss the work with them. The sale of your work is left to someone who doesn't have the knowledge of or interest in it that you do.

Though you don't have to deal with buyers, you still must conduct business with the gallery, including negotiating written contracts, collecting payment from sales, maintaining accurate records, and tracking the sale of reproduction rights.

Having your paintings in a gallery can also tie them up at a time when another market might have provided a buyer. Your sales depend on the gallery's personnel, marketing/promotion efforts, and advertising. Some galleries restrict other sales. Some galleries demand exclusive representation for a large geographical area or on all of your work.

Also, some galleries hold frequent artist receptions, robbing you of valuable creative time. Some ask the artist to partially pay for receptions and advertising, an investment you could put toward your own marketing and promotion endeavors.

If success arrives through a gallery, that director will want you to keep producing because you're bringing income into the business. This pressure to consistently replace sold works with new ones causes some artists to feel creatively stifled.

How Retail Galleries Operate

Galleries conduct business with artists in one of two ways: consignment or outright purchase.

Consignment is the method frequently chosen by galleries. In a consignment situation, artwork is hung with no exchange of money between the gallery and the artist. When a work sells, the gallery takes a percentage of the selling price (its *commission*) and the artist receives the remaining amount. If a work doesn't sell, no money is exchanged.

Galleries favor consignment because there's no initial outlay of money to build up stock and none is directly lost on unsold works. The artist and gallery share the risk.

The gallery's commission from consigned works pays its bills — utilities, rent, salaries, advertising, and so on. Commission rates vary, but an average range for retail galleries is 30 to 50 percent, normally taken on the retail, or selling, price of the work. For example, a painting retails for $125; the gallery's commission is 40 percent. When the work sells, the gallery receives 40 percent of $125 (125 multiplied by .40), which equals $50; the artist receives the remaining money (125 minus 50), which is $75.

Suppose, however, you want to have $125 in hand after the work sells. You must set the retail price high enough to reflect the subtraction of the gallery's commission so that when 40 percent is taken away, you're left with $125. To arrive at this new number, subtract the percentage of the gallery's commission from 100 percent to find out what percentage you'll receive. In this case, you'll be receiving 60 percent of the retail price (100 minus 40 = 60). Now divide the amount of money you want to have by the percentage ($125 divided by .60) — the result is your retail price ($208.33, which rounds off to $208). To check yourself, see what 40 percent (the gallery's commission) of this retail price equals and subtract it from the retail price ($208 multiplied by .40 equals $83.20). Round that off to $83 and subtract it from $208, and you're left with $125 — the amount you want after the gallery takes its commission.

Remember that when a gallery handles your works on consignment, the works are still yours, not the gallery's, until they are sold. Safeguards to protect your works while in the gallery's possession must be a part of your written artist-gallery agreement. You need to have a clear written understanding about insurance, price reductions, time payments, rentals, payment, shipping costs, and protection from loss of your works should the gallery declare bankruptcy. You also need a clear record of which paintings the gallery holds and which have sold. These points are discussed in Chapter 6.

If a gallery buys outright, it will probably request a wholesale price from you; that is, a price which it can comfortably double and still sell the work. The advantage to outright purchase is that you get paid immediately, whether or not the work ever sells from the gallery. Unfortunately, you usually don't have a say in setting the retail price, and the gallery, now the owner of the work, is not obligated to tell or ask you.

Whether the gallery sells on consignment or outright, there are several aspects of the gallery you should consider before signing a contract.

■ *Exhibitions and Shows.* The number of exhibitions/shows a gallery offers varies widely. A gallery might give a one-person show, group show, artists' reception to open the show, scheduled artists' receptions, demonstration opportunities, or nothing at all. Commonly, as one or more artists are added to a gallery, it holds a show to acquaint its clients and the public with the work it handles.

Receptions give the interested public a chance to meet the creator of the works. Some artists love receptions; others hate them. You encounter a range of reactions from attendees — gushing enthusiasm, sincere appreciation, blatant dislike — and must be prepared to meet them with tact. But overall, if a gallery offers to hold a reception in your honor, it's a real bonus. It not only gets you and your work noticed, but brings in new potential gallery clients.

Ask the gallery director if shows or receptions are given for the artists the gallery handles. If the director states that the gallery does, be sure this point is in your written gallery contract. Though an exact date might not be set, your contract should state that one show (reception) is to be held within so many weeks of your work being hung. Request notification time so you have an ample period in which to select, frame, and clean works for the show.

Some galleries request that an artist pay part of the show's expenses. If this is a condition, be certain you have a clear understanding of precisely which expenses you are responsible for and know what is being purchased. You might be willing to spring for the food, until you find out it's expensive imported wine, Brie cheese and caviar.

■ *Artist Promotion.* When a gallery agrees to handle your works, you should not assume the gallery will advertise and promote your art. It's wise to find out before a contract is signed exactly what type of promotion a gallery offers.

Some galleries are satisfied to be sleepy, out-of-the-way places that rely on serendipity for sales. Others flood newspapers with ads, sponsor art fairs, feature a new artist monthly, and commission salespeople to approach interior decorators and building contractors. Between these two extremes is the most common promotional approach. Ask the gallery director to detail his or her advertising and promotion tactics. A gallery that can't communicate an advertising budget or plan that includes you cannot be counted on to give you much recognition; weigh this factor when deciding to sign on.

■ *Exclusive Representation.* Many galleries request some form of exclusive representation of their artists. A good idea? Debatable at best, at least from your point of view.

There are two types of exclusivity—by geography and by sales. Geographical exclusivity is the most common. In this instance, the gallery wants to be the only gallery to sell your work within a certain geographical region—a few blocks' radius around the gallery, a city, a county, a whole state, or even an entire region of the country. A gallery might also interpret geographical exclusivity to mean it's to be the *only* sales outlet within that geographical area. If an interior decorator, for example, also wants to handle your work, the gallery might refuse and point to its exclusive representation agreement.

Therefore, before agreeing to any geographic exclusivity to your work, understand and write out the exact parameters of the request. Be aware that the more exclusivity you grant to one gallery, the more it restricts where you can sell your work.

The advantage to geographical exclusivity is that for that particular region, you are dealing with only one gallery, simplifying business dealings and record-keeping. The disadvantage is that if the gallery isn't promoting or selling your work, you can't go elsewhere until your contract expires.

Another type of exclusivity is exclusive sales representation, i.e., a gallery wants a commission on *all* of your sales, even those you make from your studio. I do not advise exclusive sales representation unless you *want* to turn your entire career over to a gallery and have great faith in the gallery's ability to sell and promote your artwork.

Any time a gallery requests some type of exclusive representation, be sure both you and the director clearly understand the terms and write them into your artist-gallery contract. (Refer to Chapter 6, pages 98-103, for advice on what to include in your contract.) Don't accept any exclusivity you're uncomfortable with, and understand the consequences on your sales activity.

CO-OP GALLERIES

Co-op or membership galleries are similar to retail galleries except that business aspects are shared among many people. In order to hang your work in a co-op gallery, you must contribute to the maintenance of the gallery space. Well-run co-ops enable new artists beginning to show their work to get feedback, and keep established artists in the public eye. They also offer you the chance to exchange ideas with other artists and to appreciate the problems gallery directors deal with.

Co-ops might be started by an existing artists' organization or simply by a group of artists who want to provide an exhibit space for their works. Co-ops, like retail galleries, appear in all shapes and sizes. Large ones often elect boards of directors and assign committees to handle everything from paying the rent to jurying new artists. Small ones may work with only elected officials to assign duties while

A COOPERATIVE EFFORT

Linnea Johnson, a self-taught artist from Port Angeles, Washington, says, "The hardest part of promoting my artwork was to get out and start promoting myself. Overcoming that initial fear of being rejected was a quantum leap."

Johnson has been painting seriously since 1984, but she took a major step in 1987 when she joined the local art league. Hanging her works in its co-op gallery gave Johnson that initial push and confidence she needed. "The art league members are such a nice group of people that I discovered it wasn't all that scary to talk to people. They're so interested in art and the people who do it."

Now she actively promotes herself and her work. "It's actually a lot easier than I thought. I go to all the art show openings I can, introduce myself and talk to people. If they ask if I paint, I tell them; if not, that's fine."

Believing that it's beneficial to give as well as receive, Johnson volunteers her talent and efforts to the league. "I make time for all the projects they need me for, such as coordinating the co-op gallery sitters, being assistant superintendent for the fine arts exhibit at the county fair, designing graphics for posters and announcements, donating paintings for door prizes, and so on. The moral support the league members have given me has been priceless."

everyone wears many hats to keep the gallery functioning. Some feature an artist every month with a show and reception; others primarily offer hanging space.

Keep in mind that most co-op structures require members to live within commuting distance in order to fulfill their gallery responsibilities. Some co-ops, however, allow an artist who can't give actual time to pay a fee instead. Search for a co-op that meets your specific needs.

Since co-op galleries cater to their members' works, they often feature a wide range of styles and prices. But, depending on their size and reputation, co-ops can restrict the type and size of works and the professional levels of members. Some even remove an artist's work from the gallery if the membership believes the quality has fallen. If you're still interested in joining after visiting a co-op gallery, talk with a member to learn the jurying process, what duties are required, and the amount of membership fees.

Co-op galleries also take a commission on the sale of your work in order to meet overhead expenses, but it's often much less than that taken by retail galleries. Consider joining a co-op if you want to learn more about how a gallery operates, if you like to work with other artists, and if you want an exhibit space over which you have more control.

RENTAL GALLERIES

A rental gallery, also called a vanity gallery, is gallery space that an artist rents. The gallery owner normally does nothing more for you while you pay for the space and hold your own show.

This is the least desirable of gallery situations because you foot all the bills and provide your own promotion. People in the art community avoid rental galleries because they frequently exhibit unskilled work. Rental spaces associated with museums possess more credibility, but even this depends on the criteria the museum sets regarding who can rent the space.

Occasionally you'll hear of an artist who is "discovered" because he held his own show, just as there are famous authors who started out by publishing their own books. In the long run, however, the chance is slim. Your money is better spent on your own marketing and self-promotional materials.

SHOPS

A shop frequently blends fine art paintings with its other items to offer a range of articles and prices to customers. Shops run the gamut in type and variety. Some follow a specific theme, such as nautical, Early American, or Western, but there are also those that handle any type of handmade item, be it fine art or craft, and some sell gifts and souvenirs as well.

Shops are especially advantageous to you if:

- You are fairly prolific in your art production.
- Your work tends to be smaller.
- You are looking for sales, not personal career involvement.
- Your work revolves around a particular theme. For example, you might approach a nautical shop if you paint seascapes. Rather than being limiting, "theme" shops give you exposure to an already interested audience.
- If your work falls into the low-to-middle price range, shops are a viable outlet. They frequently cater to tourists or the "average" buyer, people who purchase on impulse or are budget conscious.

The disadvantage to shops is that the owners usually don't promote artists individually. There are exceptions, of course, but promotion isn't as extensive as at a gallery.

Another disadvantage is that your work can be treated just like any other inventory item and haphazardly stored or displayed, leading to damage, loss, or inadequate viewing.

Shop owners, especially those who don't handle many one-of-a-kind items, might not be familiar with a consignment contract or understand the time and effort that went into a work. In these cases, it's especially important for you to be prepared with a written contract spelling out exactly what can and cannot be done with your work.

How Shops Operate

If a survey was taken, I'd bet that shops are split almost 50-50 as to whether artwork is handled on consignment or bought wholesale. Many shops buy work outright because the shop has more freedom to treat the work as inventory; just as many, however, handle artwork on consignment to save capital.

All of the information covering galleries (see pages 13-16) regarding consignment and outright purchase applies here. Shop owners pay more attention to a work's retail price, but this is to your advantage if your object is a sale—works will be priced to meet the customers' ability to pay.

If a shop owner is purchasing your works outright, he probably anticipates doubling the wholesale price. If you're having difficulty reaching the shop's price range but otherwise want your work sold here, consider whether you can get your desired exposure while meeting the price range. Then look at ways to keep your prices lower. Offer works matted, but not framed. Do you have very small works that are suitable? Can you offer mechanically reproduced prints, retailing for much less than an original? Ask the advice of the shop owner, make your desire to sell in his shop known, and work with him toward an equitable solution.

Good shop owners know their types of customers and what will and won't appeal to them. Their livelihood depends on understanding the spending habits and thinking of the people who shop there. Talk with the shop owner about his customers to help you to determine if your work can sell there. Perhaps some of your work is appropriate while other pieces belong elsewhere.

BOOTH SHOWS

In a booth show, you virtually run your own gallery for a day or two. You pay a fee for space and time, and then are essentially on your own. Indeed, some artists realize *all* their sales from both indoor and outdoor shows, following a planned circuit several months out of the year.

The greatest advantage to a booth show is your complete control of sales. Here you can talk about your work, get enormous exposure, hear feedback from the public, and tap in on potential future sales by obtaining names and addresses of people interested enough in your work to be on your mailing list. Gallery personnel frequent booth shows to view available talent, and sometimes indulge in networking by recommending an artist to another gallery director. A great camaraderie often builds among booth show participants, especially if they meet repeatedly on a circuit, providing you with the opportunity to network and share technical and professional knowledge.

The primary disadvantage to booth shows is the amount of preparation involved. Before you sign up for a show, be prepared in the following areas:

Sufficient Inventory: Because you're running a temporary gallery, bring a solid inventory of completed works. Count on sales being made; when they are, be prepared to hang another work in the empty space. Offer items in different price ranges to attract the most customers. If many of your works are framed watercolors ranging from $125 to $500, consider the customer who can't afford to spend that amount right now. Perhaps offer mechanical reproductions of one or two of your works for $25, unframed matted works in a bin, stationery with simple handpainted designs for $10, notecards for $1.25 apiece, or bookmarks for $1. Supply your booth with an "impulse buy" item—be sure a business card goes with these items and discuss your larger works with all buyers.

Display: Normally you are required to supply panels, screen, pegboard, or some means by which to hang the artwork. If you don't already own a display, look for ideas from other show artists. Build or buy a display system that is collapsible for hauling, sturdy enough to withstand jarring and weather, light enough to be raised alone, heavy enough to hold your largest works, and attractive. Displays can be purchased ready-made. (Art magazines, especially those listing exhibitions and shows, such as *The Artist's Magazine* and *American Artist*, carry ads for display suppliers.) Know beforehand if the sponsor expects you to provide a table for small items.

Business: Arrive at the show with bills of sale, a bank check policy firmly in mind, change for cash sales, business cards, free promotional materials for the public, business certificate with tax identification number, wrapping materials or bags (if necessary), tape, and price tags. Go over a typical sale in your mind; anticipate other needs. Arrange with a friend, relative, or the sponsor for a booth sitter, so the booth is tended when you're away. Some artists also provide a guest book for the public to sign—this becomes a mailing list for show invitations and announcements.

Emergencies: In outdoor shows, weather can change quickly. A tarpaulin roof protects your work from rain and sun, plastic sheets cover bins and provide a "break" if wind threatens to take away the inventory. Show sponsors usually won't accept responsibility for damage to your work or injury to your customers. Make sure your insurance protects against these circumstances, and also against theft.

Meeting the Public: For some, this is as easy as breathing; for others it takes positive thinking. Be friendly, smile, and don't be afraid to make an initial statement about your work. Be open to questions and out where people can see you. Make them glad they stopped at your booth, whether they buy or not. Future sales and gallery affiliations often begin with a good impression at a booth show.

If you're trying booth shows for the first time, start locally. Once you get your feet wet and decide that booth shows suit your needs, expand statewide or regionally—establish a circuit within a comfortable driving distance that potentially permits the number of desired sales.

How Booth Shows Operate

Rules governing booth shows vary from sponsor to sponsor, so it's important to send for the show's prospectus which lists the requirements and deadlines you must meet.

General practice is that most shows require a preliminary screening or judging just for acceptance into the show, that is, to be allowed to have a booth space. Usually, you submit slides (normally three to five), and the show's sponsor or a panel of judges screens them. This screening process (also called prejudging, prejurying, or entry judging) is done either to assure a balanced show (an appealing mixture of art/craft types) or to maintain a certain professional level to the entries. Sometimes in addition to slides of your artwork, a slide of your booth set-up is requested.

An entry fee, also called a prejudging,

screening, or handling fee, is usually required to accompany your slides and entry form. This fee is separate from your booth fee and generally is nonrefundable, because it defrays the cost of handling and viewing entries.

When you're accepted into the show, you're required to pay the booth fee (also called a space fee), which can range from as little as $10 for a local school-sponsored show to over $1,000 for large trade shows. Some shows, however, request all money upfront with the entry form. In these cases, the booth fee is refunded if you're rejected.

Booth spaces normally range from 10'x10' to 10'x 20', but this varies, depending on space restrictions and the number of participants. Some shows will allow you to apply for a double space to increase your exhibition area. Booth fees are often refundable up until a certain number of weeks prior to the show, but check carefully—some sponsors will not return a booth fee under any circumstances once you've paid it.

Some show sponsors take a commission on all sales; many don't. Those that do usually try to keep down the cost of the booth space in return for the additional money you're paying. You are responsible for all of your lodging, food, and mileage expenses. If the state you're in has a sales tax, you might have to apply for a temporary or transient business license. Some show sponsors anticipate this situation and are prepared with a tax ID number for you to use, collecting the sales taxes from you after the show closes.

It's your responsibility for booth set-up and dismantling, and in some shows this is a nightly obligation if the show is not indoors and guarded. Many sponsors stipulate that artists must stay the specified number of show days and may not dismantle their booths before the scheduled closing time. Many sponsors provide electricity to booths, but rental charges for other equipment, such as tables, chairs, and drapings, are common. Insurance on damage or theft of items is usually the artist's responsibility.

The manner in which you conduct your sales is normally left up to you, but hopefully the sponsors will check with you just to see how things are going and if any problems are being encountered. Some sponsors, in order to improve their shows, ask artists to evaluate the show once it's over.

JURIED ART COMPETITIONS

Juried art competitions offer awards and monetary prizes, but the artwork is not necessarily for sale. It's the prestige of winning an award that's the primary goal; the award affirms your reputation as an artist and increases your art's marketability. Juried art competitions present the opportunity for financial reward, commissions, an ego boost, and the chance to see your work in relation to others'. Some sales *do* occur through competitions, of course, but a competition should be thought of primarily as an adjunct to sales and not as a sole marketing area where sales are to be the primary goal.

The sponsor for juried art competitions is frequently a museum, art organization, corporation, or civic/government group. Awards can be ribbons, cash, purchase awards, and/or inclusion in an exhibit (traveling or stationary) and the competition catalog. These last two items offer exposure in cities and states where your work would not otherwise be seen.

The disadvantages to juried art competitions are that you lack control over the decisions made regarding your work, you may not understand the judges' thinking, and you may endure repeated rejections, which can be expensive.

In this type of competition, you submit your entry and wait. If your work isn't accepted or doesn't win an award, it's unlikely you'll ever know why. For some artists this is extremely frustrating, especially when works which are accepted or win awards appear to be of comparable quality.

If you're new at having your artwork judged, begin with local competitions. By starting locally, you get a feel for the ups and downs of competitions but probably won't have to deal with exacting shipping and packing details, restrictive size limitations, or precise framing/hanging requirements, thus making it less of a chore to enter. You'll see firsthand how your professional level compares with others' and

COMPETITIONS REAP MANY REWARDS

Susan Greaves' accomplishments include acceptance into numerous competitions, including the Audubon Artists Annual Exhibition in New York City, the Women's National Competition and Exhibition at Gallerie Triangle in Washington, D.C., the Catharine Lorillard Wolf Annual Exhibition at the National Arts Club, and the Salmagundi Exhibition for Non-Members in New York. She includes among her twenty-eight awards the John R. Grabach Memorial Award at the American Artists Professional League Show in New York, and two first place awards at the National Western Small Painting Show in New Mexico. She was featured in the "Emerging Artists" section of *American Artist* in August 1988.

Her philosophy toward entering competitions is simple and direct:

"You don't have to list on your resume the number of competitions you've entered and been rejected by; you just list the ones you got accepted to and won awards in. So the more you enter, the better chance you have to add to your resume, the better your resume becomes. I really believe galleries look at that, and I know *American Artist* did. I think it's really worth it to participate in competitions."

Susan Greaves coordinates her entire marketing package around a distinctive palette-and-brush logo set off by a clever use of graphic line. This stationery is a neutral beige-gray with deep burgundy printing. Greaves visited galleries on a recent trip to Carmel, and brought along a notebook filled with her materials in plastic-covered pages—her resume typed on letterhead, a short biography, a description of her work, and a series of pages of photographs of her paintings followed by a price list. "I also had slides, a little slide viewer, and photocopies of a few newspaper articles and exhibition notices." Though Greaves didn't get gallery representation in Carmel, California, "the directors reacted very positively to the way I presented myself."

be able to analyze where you stand—at least within your own community.

As you gain self-confidence, reputation, and artistic skill, take the risk of entering state, regional, and national competitions. When competing in a larger arena, the number and skill of the artists increase until, at the national level, you are competing against top artists from across the country.

How Competitions Operate

In most competitions, artists submit slides (or in some cases, the original work) to be juried for acceptance into the show; this is often called a prejudging. The usual request is for three to five slides and they must be *excellent*—the slides alone represent your work, talent, and skill.

A prejudging (or entry) fee is normally required to accompany the slides. In some instances, especially in local competitions, there are no entry fees, but these occasions are disappearing. If your work is accepted and the prejudging has been done from slides, then original work is requested. Judging for awards and prizes is done from the original works. Sometimes the same jurors who judge acceptance also jury for awards, but frequently award judging is performed by an entirely different person or panel, generally persons of some repute in the art field.

If your work is rejected for acceptance into a competition, your slides are usually returned accompanied by a rejection letter. Winners of prizes and awards are commonly notified soon after the judging; some competitions send out letters to all accepted artists listing award-winners' names.

COMMISSIONS

In this context, commissions don't refer to the money taken by shops and galleries. Instead, they're sales opportunities—clients request that a particular painting be created by you for their purchase.

If you specialize in human or animal portraiture, you may be accustomed to handling commissions—clients request that you paint their loved ones or pets. But other commission opportunities also exist. Perhaps someone wants a painting of his home or an artwork to fit a special room, such as one of a particular landscape, flower or scene. The possibilities are as endless as are people with desires.

Commissions can be tricky—you're painting for *one* client. You must be sure that the client will like the painting so you are paid when it's finished. There are several ways to avoid the pitfall of a client refusing to buy the finished work:

- Use a two-step contract as described in detail in Chapter 6.
- Listen attentively and take notes when the client tells you his desires.
- Be an artist who can take at least a minimum of direction. The nature of a commission means that your artistic freedom is coupled with client wishes. The two must work hand-in-hand to reach the desired end-product.
- Be certain the client has seen your previous work. It's amazing the number of people who commission a painting based on an artist's reputation without ever viewing his work. Be sure the client reviews some of your previous paintings even if only through slides or photographs.

Commissions offer the advantage of a client coming to you, so you don't have to sell your work on the open market. A commission's disadvantage is that you paint to please someone else, not necessarily yourself; some artists consider this an impossible condition to work under.

ALTERNATIVE OUTLETS

The market areas just described are the primary outlets to which artists turn to sell their works. But there are many others—usually local—that don't quite follow the traditional path. Use as many or few as you wish to reach your sales goals.

Home Studio Shows

A home studio show opens your home and/or studio to the public for a day or two for an exhibition of artworks with a reception. In effect, your home/studio becomes a temporary retail gallery, except that only your works are on display.

The advantages to a home studio show are that you reap all of the profit from sales—there's no one to pay a commission to; there's minimal, if any, transportation of works; and you have complete control over the hanging/display of works, sales terms, and exhibition hours.

The greatest drawback to a home studio show is the amount of time and attention to detail needed to prepare for it. First and foremost, you need adequate space so that viewers can see your works without distraction. This might mean thoroughly cleaning your studio, disrupting family areas of your home, or cleaning out your garage. Besides physical space for your paintings, you need: adequate parking; a solid inventory of completed works; a mailing list with enough names to make your time/money investment worthwhile; printed invitations addressed and mailed at least two weeks prior to the show; adequate food and drink in a space slightly away from your artwork to avoid accidental damage; helpers, so that you can meet and talk with potential clients while others replenish refreshments or handle the paperwork for sales; bills of sale; and promotional brochures or flyers and business cards so attendees take something home with them to remind them of your name and work.

Consider holding a home studio show with two or three other artists. Split the costs evenly and have each artist responsible for her sales. Mailing lists can be combined and the preparation tasks divided equally so that all the work doesn't fall to one person.

Places of Business

Many businesses will agree to hang your works, either for free or for a small commission. Consider bookstores, medical offices, insurance firms, real estate offices, department stores, boutiques, theater lobbies, furniture or interior decorators' showrooms, hotel lobbies, banks, savings and loans, restaurants, printers, indeed, any local business that attracts the clientele you want to reach and has sufficient wall space.

If artists' works are already present, find out the name of the person in charge of the display and learn their rules and practices regarding the handling of artists' works.

If no artistic original works are present, but you believe your works are perfect for the available space, meet with the person in charge of the business and/or building. Explain why your art is suitable, how original works can benefit his business and work environment, and how easily and equitably the arrangements can be handled. Bring examples of your work so the owner can see exactly the type of work you do. You'll need:

- A written contract so there's no misunderstanding about the commission, hanging time, hanging arrangement, promotional materials, or insurance.
- Time to check these establishments to make sure your work is not being defaced, lost, or mishandled and that your business card, name plates, price tags, and promotional materials are adequately stocked and attached.
- A firm understanding about how sales should be handled.

Institutions and Centers

Many times both private and public institutions want artwork to help brighten and enhance the environment but don't have the money to purchase permanent works. Some institutions, especially colleges, universities, and libraries support exhibits of local artists and even provide gallery space. Talk with the directors of local institutions about hanging your work in their buildings. You'll need a written contract similar in points to the one written for small businesses and, if your work is not in an actual gallery space, you'll need to invest the same amount of time to check up on your art. Libraries, colleges, universities, high schools, senior citizen centers, hospitals, counseling centers, rehabilitation centers, and recreation centers are good places to contact.

FINE ART AS GRAPHIC ART

Both local and national sales opportunities exist in the graphic arts field for fine artists, especially in art publishing, greeting card publishing, and editorial usage.

When you first approach a graphic arts field, be prepared to confront a slightly different attitude than what you're accustomed to in the fine arts field. Graphic art buyers definitely view your work for its potential as a printed and salable product.

When you mail slides or photographs, or attend in-person reviews, you're showing these buyers samples of your skill and talent. The buyers may or may not actually buy the right to reproduce one of the works you submit. Instead, these samples are often used only to give them an idea of what you do. They will call with an assignment for creation of a specific artwork.

Many times, especially in mailed submissions, these sample slides/photographs are filed by art buyers as reminders of an artist's interest and talent. If you meet buyers in person, leave one to three slides/photographs for their files. Clearly label your slides/photographs and make sure your printed promotional pieces list your phone number. Do not expect them to be returned—you want the buyer to file them and keep you in mind for assignments.

Art Publishers

Art publishers are those firms that pay you for the right to reproduce your painting(s) as either limited or unlimited edition prints. Some publishers specialize in one subject area, style, or medium, but all want appealing, salable images. These are often subjects with mass appeal, colors that complement neutral decorating colors, and images that can be easily seen, even across a room.

When dealing with art publishers, always have a written contract and be sure you understand:

- Exactly which painting(s) is to be reproduced.
- The number of reproductions in an edition.
- Reproduction right(s) sold.
- Payment method (flat fee or royalty).
- Payment date or schedule.
- Who pays shipping costs.

- Amount of insurance coverage while at the printer/publisher.
- The extent of the publisher's responsibility for printing, distribution, and promotion.
- Mandatory artist credit and placement of your copyright notice on the reproductions.
- Conditions under which your paintings may be cropped or changed.

Greeting Card Publishers

This vast field is always open to images that appeal emotionally to people, especially to women, who buy the majority of greeting cards. It's often the artwork on a card that compels a buyer to pick it up and the verse that clinches the sale.

Some firms specialize in cards for particular seasons, such as Christmas or Easter, or in one genre, such as religious cards. Visit card shops and stationery stores to see if your artwork fits the style of a particular company's cards.

As with art publishers, always have a written contract that covers:

- Exactly which painting is being reproduced.
- What reproduction right(s) are sold.
- Payment method (flat fee or royalty).
- Payment schedule.
- Who pays shipping costs.
- The amount of insurance coverage while the painting is at the company.
- Mandatory artist credit and copyright notice.
- Requirement that no cropping or change take place in your painting without notification and your permission. Please note, however, that it's not unusual, because of the standard size of greeting card illustrations (5″x7″ or 6″x8″) for artworks to be reduced to fit proportionally to the card. If your work is not already in proportion to these standard card sizes, some cropping is going to take place. Let the publisher know you're aware of this possibility and that you'd like to be informed regarding the amount and position of the cropping prior to printing.

MARKETING OPPORTUNITIES EXIST EVERYWHERE

California artist Anita Neal's background in marketing and business has given her fresh ideas on where and how to market artwork. Her advice to artists is: "Utilize all the places you and your friends do business. Ask to display your work in these places. Contact doctors, dentists, printers, boutiques, dress shops, hobby shops, department stores. Go into business centers and speak to the property managers. Go to business offices, real estate offices and escrow companies. As you talk to these people, always ask if they know of someone you might contact for your art.

"Have churches, business organizations, and service clubs sponsor a fundraising event. Donate some of your work and do the publicity and promotion for recognition.

"Have a friend give you a reception in her home. Display your art throughout, especially in the bathrooms, entrance and kitchen. Put up plywood or plasterboard panels along two or three sides of the garage and hang your work. The best time for a reception is on Sunday between 2 and 4 P.M. or Saturday between 7 and 9 P.M.

"Band a group of artist friends together and create your own show or exhibition. Pool talents and share the cost of the opening. Print and send out invitations and press releases, with photos if possible. Prepare a map of your respective studios/homes and plan a stop-to-stop progression for the prospective art buyers. At the first stop, have a price list with each artist's name *boldly* printed at the top of the page and hand this to buyers as they arrive. It's also important to have each person sign a guest book; make photocopies for each participating artist later. Be certain all exhibited artworks are accompanied by a label listing the work's title and price."

If the artwork is an assignment, also cover:

- The parameters of the project (exactly what you are to produce).
- Deadline for final art.
- Change or kill fees. If the buyer wants changes in your "final" art or the project is terminated, you should be reimbursed for the time and money you've invested.

Editorial Usage

Books, magazines, newsletters, and newspapers all need art to accompany written text. Paintings frequently become covers or full-page illustrations.

Contact publications that seem most suited to your artwork. For example, if you paint florals, contact gardening and flower publications. The more you focus your marketing, the better.

It's more likely that you'll receive an assignment rather than sell a painting you have already completed, since editorial needs change with each publication. If you're an artist who can visually interpret the written word, bring this to the attention of the buyer.

The contract points listed for greeting card publishers apply here.

Some other graphic arts buyers to consider are:

- Needlecraft manufacturers.
- Local business/government.
- Church and organization publications.
- T-shirt designs.
- Calendar companies.
- Advertising agencies.
- Public relations firms.
- Catalog publishers.
- Local printers (supplying art for clients' projects).

For more information about graphic arts markets and how to contact them, read *The Graphic Artist's Guide to Marketing and Self-Promotion* and *Artist's Market.*

CHAPTER TWO
CHECKLISTS

Markets available to fine artists:
- ☐ Galleries
- ☐ Shops
- ☐ Booth shows
- ☐ Juried art competitions
- ☐ Commissions
- ☐ Alternative markets
- ☐ Graphic art markets

Galleries offer many benefits, such as:
- ☐ Adding to your reputation
- ☐ Increasing your exposure
- ☐ Offering exhibitions and shows
- ☐ Offering advertising and artist promotion

However, galleries have their drawbacks, such as:
- ☐ Reducing your opportunity to talk with buyers and to control sales
- ☐ Possibly limiting sales opportunities through exclusive representation
- ☐ Possibly closing on short notice or going bankrupt

There are many advantages to selling your work in shops:
- ☐ Especially advantageous to prolific artists
- ☐ Generally aren't involved directly with your career
- ☐ Prices are usually in the low-to-middle range

Shops also have their drawbacks:
- ☐ Seldom offer receptions, exhibitions, shows
- ☐ Seldom promote or advertise individual artists
- ☐ Can close abruptly or go bankrupt
- ☐ Fine art works might not receive special handling

Some of the advantages of selling your work in booth shows are:
- ☐ Booths offer complete control of sales to artist
- ☐ They offer exposure to gallery contacts

☐ Booths provide more opportunities to network with other artists

Booths require adequate preparation:
- ☐ Bring sufficient inventory
- ☐ Provide your own display apparatus
- ☐ Supply your own business transaction materials
- ☐ Prepare for weather changes and emergency situations

Juried art competitions offer:
- ☐ Awards, sometimes money, and the possibility of exhibition and catalog exposure
- ☐ A boost to your reputation

Drawbacks to juried art competitions include:
- ☐ Insufficient sales opportunities to be primary marketing outlet
- ☐ No artist control over acceptance or rejection

For a commission, a client requests you to create a specific piece or pieces. When considering this offer, remember to:
- ☐ Show the client your previous work
- ☐ Use a two-step contract
- ☐ Listen to the client's wishes
- ☐ Be flexible

Alternative markets include:
- ☐ Businesses
- ☐ Lobbies
- ☐ Professionals' offices
- ☐ Institutions and centers
- ☐ Home studio shows

Fine artists find the following graphic art markets profitable:
- ☐ Art publishers
- ☐ Greeting card publishers
- ☐ Magazines
- ☐ Book publishers

CHAPTER 3

MARKETING AND SELF-PROMOTION

What is marketing and self-promotion? Marketing is placing your artwork in the marketplace for sale. Self-promotion is promoting yourself and your work, not necessarily for immediate sale, but to enhance and build your reputation and to familiarize people with you and your work.

Any marketing effort has three goals: to inform a potential consumer of the product's existence; to show how the product meets the consumer's desires; and to inform the consumer where and how the product can be purchased.

The following six marketing steps outline how to sell your work directly and economically. The first three gather information; the next three initiate action. Read through them carefully; they're vital to your success.

First, analyze your product. You need to know exactly what it is you're trying to sell — all good salespeople know their products inside and out. Analysis also clarifies your "sales" personality.

Second, determine the actual market areas appropriate for your work. This is accomplished by understanding your product, your personality, and the goals you've set for your career. This combination of your unique information clarifies the market areas you should — and shouldn't — approach now.

Third, locate potential clients. Researching names and addresses of potential clients within specific markets refines marketing efforts and lessens the hit-and-miss aspect of marketing. Rejection is reduced because you're zeroing in on those clients most open to your type of work.

Fourth, develop your marketing strategy and tools. Keep yourself on the road to success by developing marketing tools focused on your chosen market areas that present your work in its most accurate and compelling light.

Fifth, initiate your marketing plan. Utilizing the knowledge of your product, specific market areas, focused marketing tools, and client list, maintain a marketing calendar and write out definite short- and long-range mar-

keting goals. This is your individual road map heading you directly toward your destination.

Sixth, evaluate and update your marketing efforts. As your career grows and evolves, your marketing and self-promotion must do the same. Review your printed materials and target market(s) to keep your marketing efforts fresh.

Now we'll detail these steps one by one.

STEP ONE: ANALYZING YOUR ART PRODUCT

It might sound silly to analyze your art product — after all, you know what you create. But this step is much more than saying "I think this one will sell, but this one won't." Why? Because your art product is both you and your artwork, not just the finished work. An artist and his creations are inextricably united. Until you have a firm knowledge of the type of artwork you create best and that which you sincerely like to create, until you understand who you are as an artist today by seeing how you've evolved, you aren't going to know the art product you're marketing.

This doesn't mean you are locked into creating only one "salable" type, style, or subject matter. Rather, this process should help you pick out those you've been the most artistically successful with and then to go one step further to understanding why. It initiates insight into your artistic self and forces you to review your career — high and low points alike — to see what led to each.

The questions provided here are only guides, "triggers," if you will, to get you started with your own artist-specific analysis.

The Analysis Process

Grant yourself several hours of quiet and line your studio with as much of your work — old and new — as is reasonable in a general chronological order. Sit in the center with a pad and pen. If actual works aren't available, sit with slides or photographs of your works.

Start with your oldest works and make notes on the subject matter, medium, technique and style, and one or two words on how you feel about that work now. Move on gradually to your newest works until all have been covered.

Now answer these questions:

■ Has my subject matter changed? If it has, have I randomly gone through subjects or is there a thread of continuity running through each, such as a study of light and shadow, color or composition? Can I pull the knowledge I've gained from these works to create future works?

If not, have I explored this particular subject matter to its fullest? Is it time to move on to another subject? Or is this subject still exciting to me, creating a depth of study to my work that wouldn't exist if I switched now?

What is my favorite subject matter, the one I return to again and again or receive the most pleasure or satisfaction from doing?

■ Did I switch to another medium? If I have, did this change improve my work? Have I found a medium in which I feel comfortable? If I haven't, have I become more proficient in understanding and using the medium I've stayed with? Do I understand its properties, how far it can be stretched and at what point it breaks down? Do I truly feel "at peace and at home" with this medium?

■ Have I improved my technique? Do I understand the medium I've chosen well enough to feel fairly confident as I begin a new work? Have I developed *my* way of handling the medium so I achieve desired results? Do I almost intuitively know which brush to use and how to use it to achieve the effect I want? Do I continue to read and study to improve my way of seeing color, composition and light? Do I need advancement in any of these areas?

■ Have I evolved a unique style, one that is recognizable as my own? Am I growing as an artist, adding my own flair and artistic vision? Do my paintings stand apart in some way from others? Is there an intangible quality that makes them special? Have I found a new way of seeing an old subject, a new way of using color, a new way of combining elements or using light and shadow?

■ If I've previously marketed my work and the paintings I'm reviewing are ones that didn't sell, is there any obvious reason why they didn't? Early, less professional works? Poor use of color? Lack of skill in handling medium and subject matter? Do I now feel I've overcome these prior deficiencies? If not, what can I do to change this?

As you answer these questions, write down all of the thoughts that come into your head. Your paper will gradually fill with positive and negative comments.

Take these sheets of paper and reorganize them into the two units—positive and negative. The positive aspects to your works and growth as an artist become the basis of your written text for printed marketing tools, as well as a well-deserved ego boost. Evaluate the negative aspects—has something shown up that you seriously need to work on? Can you turn the negatives into positives by taking such actions as enrolling in a drawing class, attending a workshop under a respected artist, brushing up on basics, or taking time to renew "seeing as an artist"?

You might also experience further revelations while you do this analysis. Some artists delightfully discover a greater improvement in their skill and creativity than they had suspected. This generates renewed confidence and a desire to keep working to find out what's ahead. Others discover they have been in a rut for years—little or no growth has occurred, and a "sameness" has attached itself to their works, giving the paintings a staleness the artist wasn't aware existed.

File these pages, but keep them easily accessible for future use. With this solid base of knowledge on which to build, you're ready to move on to Step Two.

STEP TWO: FINDING YOUR TARGET MARKETS

Finding your target markets involves a more detailed look at the physical properties of your artworks, your "sales" personality, the financial goals you've set for yourself, and where you'd *like* to have your work sold.

Target markets are the one or two general market "areas," discussed in Chapter 2, to which you're going to focus your marketing time, money, and effort. The other areas won't be forgotten, but by targeting, you're no longer scattering your time and energy or putting money into ineffectual generic printed materials trying to be everywhere.

Review the market areas, if necessary, then answer the following questions to help you zero in on those areas most suitable to you and your work. As you do this, some of the market areas will naturally eliminate themselves either because of the nature of the work you do or your own personality. If more than two remain as viable options when you've completed the questions, consider more heavily the potential financial returns and where you'd like to see your work to help narrow your selections.

■ Does the physical size of most of my paintings render them unsuitable for some markets? (For example, 6'x7' paintings aren't marketable in shops, most lobbies or booth shows. If you paint in this size, consider galleries, juried art competitions, commissions and some alternative markets as primary market areas.)

■ Does the subject matter of most of my paintings reduce potential outlets? (Nudes often get a cold shoulder in shops, booth shows, and some alternative markets, for example, and even some galleries won't handle them. Portraiture is unacceptable to many galleries but lends itself to commissions.) Is my subject matter so regional or esoteric that I must confine myself to one area or type of outlet? (For example, very symbolic or abstract art appeals more to avant-garde audiences of the East or West coasts than to the Midwest or Central Western states.) Which market areas are approachable in the geographical areas I'm restricted to?

■ Am I so shy that the thought of meeting a potential client in person fills me with panic? (For the time being, then, don't consider booth shows or commissions as market areas, and plan to do most of your marketing in areas easily contacted through the mail, such as graphic art markets or galleries. Many artists find that once the ice is broken and interested clients call them, the shyness disappears and in-person meetings become viable options.)

■ How am I most comfortable dealing with money? Do I want someone else to handle this aspect or do I want to be in full charge? (If you want complete control over how a sale is conducted then steer clear of market areas where others are selling your work for you.)

■ Am I willing to take direction from a client to give him the work he desires, or does it have to be my way or not at all? (If it has to be your way, don't focus on the marketing areas of commissions or graphic art markets until you believe you can be more flexible.)

■ Do I consider marketing and selling my artwork demeaning? (Better do some serious thinking about your attitude and question whether you should be marketing yet. Though not a conscious thought, this deep-seated belief can influence your whole attitude and set you up for repeated rejection or victimization. Payment for your work is truly a high compliment. As Rosalind Lipscomb says, "To me, money is like applause is to an actress.")

■ Do I become impatient, intolerant, or perhaps rude when people don't understand or appreciate my work? (Though at times understandable, a hostile attitude doesn't encourage sales. It usually stems from frustration and anger. While trying to find the roots of these feelings, turn your thinking to market areas where your type of work might find more acceptance, even if it means going outside your home area and marketing by mail.)

■ Are there market areas in which I'm familiar with the business aspects involved? (All other factors being equal, if you have more business knowledge in one area than another, lean toward the area where you're already comfortable.)

■ Which market areas at this time appear capable of offering me the financial return and/or artistic growth I'm seeking?

■ Where do I *want* my work to be sold? (Choose for now the areas where you'll feel proud and comfortable to have your work seen. Sometimes you consciously or subconsciously feel you'd rather die than have your work seen in a particular market; admit to the feeling and don't try to push yourself where you don't want to go. A new experience can change your attitude; if this occurs, then consider that market area.)

■ What type(s) of work do I most enjoy creating? (You should have a good idea from analyzing your work in Step One. There's no reason to do work that doesn't excite you just to fit a certain market area; it should be the other way around. If the work you love is slightly off the beaten path, apply marketing research principles stringently so that the markets most open to the work you love are found.)

As you worked your way through the questions, artwork and personality traits became more refined. Other factors, such as where you live, ability to travel, etc., influenced your answers. And as all of your personal information was processed, the fields *most* appropriate for you became more clear.

Following is an example of how one artist joined artwork and personality together to select the market area and method of contact she'll focus on.

Watercolorist Sandra Daily loves to render houses, and her works are of an "average" frameable size. As a bonus, she loves to meet people and easily communicates her enthusiasm for wanting them to have a portrait of their home to cherish.

Sandra should definitely make commissions her *target market*, focusing all of her marketing tools and goals to building her reputation and sales in home portraiture. While commissions grow, her secondary target market can be shops, booth shows, or alternative markets like lobbies and businesses, for display of historic buildings and area landmarks. If she lives in a small town, she might have to plan junkets to neighboring cities to build her portraiture business or develop a marketing plan where she paints from photographs. But she's focused in on her target market, commissions, and can now move ahead on her marketing plan.

What if Sandra doesn't like to meet people? Then a slight twist to her marketing plans is called for. Commissions can still be a target market, but she might have to do all of her advertising through local newspapers and national magazines and all of her painting from photographs. Booth shows are not a good option for her, and she wouldn't feel comfortable approaching business owners with her historic buildings. But she could hold a home studio show and have the support of friends nearby, or consider graphic art editorial uses for landmark paintings and do her marketing through the mail.

STEP THREE: LOCATING CLIENTS

Your body of knowledge is growing. You know your art product and your target market areas. Step three personalizes the target market by locating specific potential clients within the market.

Market research is mandatory to locate potential clients. This process is time-consuming, but vital; in it lies your best chance for success.

At this point, you want to locate a substantial number of names and addresses within a particular market area. This list will be refined later. The number of names/addresses on this initial potential client list depends on whether your marketing efforts are local or national, and the amount of time, money, and energy you can expend. If you're seeking only local clients at this time, or if your marketing efforts are restricted, then your list will be shorter than if you are open to national possibilities and full-time marketing. Begin your search with the following:

Galleries: Locally, names and addresses of art galleries are as close as the phone book's Yellow Pages and other municipal business directories. If a gallery uses a display ad, read it carefully for a one- or two-line description, such as, "specializing in watercolor," or "abstract works are our specialty." Such brief descriptions help you determine if the gallery's suitable for your work, even at this early stage of your client list.

Read the art pages of newspapers and any ads included here. Call local art associations, museums, and other artists for suggestions and recommendations. Contact your local chamber of commerce and city tourist/visitor bureau regarding the availability of a local gallery guide.

BALANCING TEACHING AND ART

Christopher Bull of Albuquerque, New Mexico, finds that two vocations—teaching and creating art—force him to be realistic about the number of galleries he can handle, limiting his marketing accordingly.

Currently a full-time art teacher, Bull wants to focus on his artwork and place it in galleries. "I want to re-emphasize that part of me. Lately I haven't been able to because I've been teaching so much. I *was* in twelve galleries from Los Angeles to Chicago, but I found I couldn't handle that many and still teach. And there's no way to keep up with that many galleries on a part-time basis. It's very time-consuming to keep in touch with them, send them new work, and so on. You either have to do it full-time or market regionally."

Bull's target market remains galleries, but his marketing will be adjusted to "several *good* galleries, not so far away." This way, "It keeps it on a manageable scale."

CHRISTOPHER BULL

For state, regional, or national marketing, obtain gallery-specific publications, such as *Art Gallery Magazine*, *Art Now USA* (the national publication), *Art Now Gallery Guides* (regional guides), and *Art in America*, to name only a few. Other state and regional guides are available; check your local library or contact the state art council in the state you're interested in. Numerous other general art publications, such as *Southwest Art*, *ARTnews*, *Art Today*, *Art West*, and *American Indian Art Magazine*, contain gallery ads. Names of other art publications can be found at your library in the *Standard Periodical Directory*, a reference book listing publications by subject.

A book devoted to galleries is *American Art Galleries: The Illustrated Guide to Their Art and Artists*, edited by Les Krantz. Here are descriptions of more than 1,000 galleries, consisting of the gallery's name, address, phone number, director, hours, types of artwork, and artists exhibited.

Libraries contain the Yellow Pages for major cities across the country, and state visitor/tourist bureaus often have compiled gallery guides, providing access to names and addresses for specific areas.

Shops: Because of the variety of shops and the differing circumstances surrounding each establishment, you should stick to local or regional businesses. You can find these in the Yellow Pages, business directories, tourist/visitor bureau guides, and chambers of commerce. Simply driving around an area that interests you elicits names and addresses, as does scanning the newspaper for shop ads.

If you're seeking special-interest shops, purchase magazines that deal with your subject, since shops often advertise to these readers.

Booth Shows: If you're starting out on a local level for your booth show, your initial list will contain only those shows within easy driving distance. Much of the time, local shows are advertised on bulletin boards, in art supply stores, art galleries, frame stores, craft stores, art association newsletters, newspaper ads, and on posters in store windows. You can also call local art associations and other artists for recommendations of shows they've participated in.

For state, regional, and national shows, read the magazines that list numerous shows, such as *American Artist*, *Sunshine Artists USA*, and *The Artist's Magazine*. Since many of these shows accept both art and craft, consider also *The Crafts Report* that boasts pages of show listings. Some state art councils and tourist/visitor bureaus also list shows, especially ones that are strong tourist attractions; regional art publications frequently advertise this information.

Juried Art Competitions: These competitions are generally found in listings in art magazines, newsletters, and regional publications; some art editors of newspapers also make it a habit to announce competitions. If you belong to a national or well-known art association or have previously entered competitions, an announcement might be mailed to you.

Commissions: This list is slightly more difficult to compile, but is likely to be delineated by economic status, residence, or area of interest. For example, everyone might love to own a watercolor portrait of their child, but not everyone can afford one. You want to reach those people who *most* readily can. Thus your research aims toward private school directories, hospital and library board lists, presidents of companies, attorneys, physicians, and so on—those people who probably are in the middle- to upper-income brackets.

To target a certain residential area, check city directories (available in most libraries), which list information alphabetically by street name, including house numbers and most residents' names.

If your commission specialty is in one area, such as dogs, find service businesses associated with this interest, in this case veterinarians, kennels, pet shops, and any organization focused on dogs. For information on associations, check the *Encyclopedia of Associations*, a multi-volume reference work that contains comprehensive listings on approximately 20,000 national and geographic organizations. Organizations are indexed alphabetically by name and key word (area of interest); there are also geographical and chief executive indexes.

This reference book can put you in touch with art-related organizations as well as the specific interest groups. Even if you aren't interested in or eligible to join, these associations can often increase your professional knowledge through services, pamphlets, newsletters, and books.

Alternative Outlets: Because these are primarily local marketing opportunities, develop your list through the Yellow Pages, business directories, newspaper ads, chambers of commerce, and by networking with local artists, art associations, and businesspersons.

Graphic Art Markets: For local art publishers, check your Yellow Pages and with galleries, museums, frame shops, art associations, and artists for suggestions and recommendations. For national listings, obtain a copy of *Decor Source Book*, which lists publishers, distributors, and suppliers. This issue is available only through Commerce Publishing Co., listed in the resource section of this book. You can also find art publishers in *Artist's Market*, a yearly directory of graphic art markets. Available in bookstores and most libraries, this book lists publishers' names, addresses, phone numbers, contact person, the type of artwork the publisher seeks, and more.

Greeting card publishers can also be found in *Artist's Market*, as well as in *Thomas Register of American Manufacturers*, a multi-volume reference work that supplies information on all U.S. businesses that manufacture a product or supply a service.

Other ways to obtain names and addresses are by looking on the backs of actual greeting cards and reading *Greetings Magazine*, a publication for the retail greeting card trade.

Editorial uses include newspapers, magazines, and books. For magazines, use *Artist's Market*, *Gale Directory of Publications*, and the *Standard Periodical Directory*. The latter two reference works divide publications by subject area and provide valuable additional information. *Writer's Market* is an annual directory of consumer publications. Listings are divided into 46 categories, according to editorial interest. There are also 70 categories of trade, technical, and professional journals.

For newspapers, research *Gale Directory of Publications* and the *Editor & Publisher Yearbook*.

A MAN OF ALL ARTS

Michaellallen McGuire, of Santa Fe, New Mexico, is a fine artist, graphic artist, and businessperson, and understands the interrelationship of the three roles in his life.

A professional artist since 1971, he's combined illustration, teaching, and fine art into a full-time career, teaching now only "to fill in the gaps." He's conducted a juggling act between graphic art and fine art for years, but now sees a steady shift toward fine art. "My life's dream has been to be a gallery painter—a fine artist—and now it's finally happening."

McGuire works primarily in oils for his gallery pieces and specializes in landscapes, birds, and wildlife. He believes fine art is more difficult to break into than graphic art. "There's a ready market for commercial art out there—it's not a luxury, it's business. People *need* the art and they'll pay for it. With fine art, you're appealing to a client's luxury income 95 percent of the time, so you're appealing to a different audience. The fine art client has tastes that are very selective, very acute, and people go to a great deal of effort to decide whether or not they want a piece."

McGuire credits his commercial art training and background with giving him skills and discipline particularly useful to fine art markets. "You learn discipline, work schedules, and to redo projects without ego, if you're intelligent enough to realize you've got to do it that way. You learn to draw and paint well in *all* media, and to do it fast. And you learn to meet production schedules.

"A gallery wants the same thing. It wants you to meet production schedules—it wants paintings in there if they're selling. And it wants good paintings; if they're not good, they'll send them back."

His business expertise was developed through college business courses, seminars, books, law study, and an understanding that "the world is not going to beat a path to your door. You're involved in the process of generating a product. Art has nothing to do with making money, but if you want to continue at painting, you have to make money to stay alive. Art has to do with all the aesthetic concepts—composition, lights, darks, contrasts, color—working the elements of art and applying them through the principles of design. These have nothing to do with making money—they're the joy of art."

But to have more time and money for the joys of art, he says, "You must be a salesperson, or somebody must sell for you. In the initial stages, everybody's a salesperson because you have to sell somebody on the idea of selling your work. Eventually a gallery takes over the selling and you're free of that responsibility. The more you sell, the more money you have, and you can start hiring others to do things, like your shipping, crating, and framing. Once again you're more free."

The knowledge that more sales equal more time to paint doesn't always ease the drudgery of the business side of his artwork. "The business of art is very time-consuming. For instance, yesterday I was my secretary for the entire day. Catching up on inventory pieces, logging in sold pieces according to purchaser, logging in pieces shipped to galleries, solicitations sent out—samples organized, assembled into envelopes, addressed, cover letters typed—the whole morning was spent typing cover letters. It's not exciting work, but it has to be done. I have these days at least once a month, and this season it's been more like once a week, because there's so much activity. I also send thank-you notes, just a personal touch that makes such a difference in my ability to continue as a businessperson."

McGuire uses one marketing tool to serve as many functions as possible. His letterhead is utilized for cover letters, short and long biography sheets, resume, inventory (consignment) sheets, and general correspondence. His brochure is being designed as a large notecard so it can also be sent like a mailer. The front will feature a color photograph of a painting, and the inside biographical material will run over a black-and-white halftone of a painting. The back will have space for a return address, stamp, and an address. It's a versatile piece, designed to get as much use as possible from one piece.

This layout of materials shows the steps McGuire took to have his business card printed. The process involved three steps. First (A), a graduated gray tone was airbrushed onto stiff board by McGuire. Second, his original artwork (B), containing his name in white on a black background, address, phone and script "Studio," sized for use as letterhead, was photostatted and reduced by 34 percent to make it appropriate for the business card. Third, burning the printing plate was completed in two operations. "First the airbrush halftone was burned in and then the hard black area was burned in over that. When it was printed, off of one plate, I had these two operations going—a nice mid-tone transitional gray and the hard black-and-white copy." The final product is a dignified and distinctive business card (C).

A

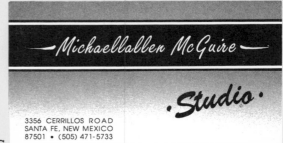

B

C

---Michaellallen McGuire---

.Studio.

3356 CERRILLOS ROAD
SANTA FE, NEW MEXICO
87501 • (505) 471-5733

D

---Michaellallen McGuire---

.Studio.

3356 CERRILLOS ROAD
SANTA FE, NEW MEXICO
87501 • (505) 471-5733

BORN	1946	Columbus, Ohio
EDUCATION	1987-88	Study with Irby Brown
	1986	Workshop with Tony Couch
	1984	Workshop with Mary DeLoyht-Arendt
	1980-82	Study with Peter Aschwanden
	1970	B.A. Degree from Ohio University
AWARDS	1988	Signature Membership in N.M. Watercolor Society (Charter Member)
	1977	"ART IN PUBLIC PLACES" Grant from New Mexico Arts Division
SPECIAL ACHEIVEMENTS	1987	Background artist for "WATCHKINS" feature-length animated film; UMA MIRAGE Productions, Austin, Texas
	1973	"CREATION COMPOSITIONS" published by M. McGuire
	1972	"COSMIC EROTICA" published by Norsidd Publishing Co., Hollywood, California
JURIED EXHIBITIONS	1988	N. M. WATERCOLORS, NMWS Signature Membership Show, Governor's Gallery
		CELEBRATION OF WATERCOLOR '88, NMWS, Alb., NM
	1987	SANTA FE FESTIVAL OF THE ARTS, Santa Fe, N.M.
		PROFESSIONAL FINE ARTS EXHIBIT, N.M. State Fair, Albuquerque, N.M.
		BELLO COLOR DE AGUA, Membership Show-New Mexico Watercolor Society; Thomson Gallery, Albuquerque, N.M.

E

---Michaellallen McGuire---

.Studio.

3356 CERRILLOS ROAD
SANTA FE, NEW MEXICO
87501 • (505) 471-5733

RESUME´ BRIEF

Michaellallen McGuire is a LANDSCAPE and WILDLIFE painter in oils and watercolors. He was born in Columbus, Ohio in 1946 and has resided in Santa Fe, New Mexico since 1974. He has taught art in various capacities and worked as a muralist for over twelve years having nine major murals in New Mexico. A signature member of the New Mexico Watercolor Society, Michaellallen also works as a free-lance illustrator and creates animation backgrounds for television and video animation.

Michaellallen currently shows at the Variant Galleries in Santa Fe and Taos, New Mexico; at the Tumbleweed Gallery in Albuquerque, New Mexico; and at the Pacific Gallery in Malibu, California.

G

McGuire used the same piece of original artwork (B) full size to reproduce as his letterhead; one piece of artwork functioned for printing two marketing materials. He chose not to place the airbrush halftone on his letterhead because it disappears as it comes down to the bottom of the business card. While looking nice on the business card, he thought the effect would be too busy for the stationery. "I believe the black-and-white images are complemented by the halftone on the business card without the entire package becoming redundant—it has a little variety." McGuire's letterhead (D) serves numerous functions: it contains his resume (E), long biographical sheet (F), and short biographical summary (G).

---Michaellallen McGuire---

.Studio.

3356 CERRILLOS ROAD
SANTA FE, NEW MEXICO
87501 • (505) 471-5733

BIOGRAPHICAL DATA SHEET

Michaellallen McGuire received his Bachelor's Degree from Ohio University in Athens, Ohio. He has taught art in various capacities including a position at the Brentwood Art Center in Los Angeles, California; two years as an art therapist at the Columbus State Mental Hospital in Columbus, Ohio; and seven years as a part-time fine arts instructor at the Santa Fe Preparatory High School in Santa Fe, New Mexico.

He has been a muralist for over twelve years having accomplished over fourteen major murals, nine of which are in New Mexico. He was awarded a grant from the New Mexico Arts Division's "Art in Public Places" project.

Michaellallen has exhibited recently at the Governors Gallery in Santa Fe, the Santa Fe Festival of the Arts, the Audubon Art Exhibition of Alaska Wildlife in Anchorage, Alaska; the National

F

© Michaellallen McGuire.
Used with permission.

For book publishers, use *Writer's Market* and *Literary Market Place*, a reference book that provides a wealth of publishing information, including publishers' names, addresses, phone numbers, and the types of books published.

DEVELOPING A CLIENT CONTACT LIST

You now have a list of names and addresses. Because you were selective about which names and addresses you wrote down, this list already reflects a targeting of likely clients. It's time to further refine this list so that the clients you contact, whether in person or by mail, are the *most* appropriate ones for your painting and career goals.

This is accomplished by finding out as much information as possible about each potential client *before* you spend the time, money, and effort on a marketing contact. This research is actually an evaluation process of the value and appropriateness of that client to you and your work, and will vary slightly from market area to market area.

To keep track of the information you obtain, fill out a 3″x5″ index card with the outlet name, address, phone number, and name of the person who reviews artists' works. After each evaluation, list on the card the facts and the opinions you form from answering the questions listed below. These records are vital, because at the end of your evaluation process, the cards of viable contacts become your *contact client list*, the list you'll work from for your actual in-person or mail solicitation. Always keep all evaluation cards, even for outlets you believe you won't be contacting. As your work evolves, these outlets may become valuable and appropriate.

Evaluating a Gallery

The best way to determine the suitablity of a gallery is to visit it in person. Visit first as an observer, not as an artist seeking a client. Be aware of your first impressions—these are likely the same impressions buyers will have when they walk through the gallery doors. Some questions to ask yourself are:

- Is the gallery easy to find? Is it located in an area of pedestrian traffic or do potential buyers have to purposely seek it out?
- How is the artwork displayed? On the walls? Sitting on the floor? Can you see each work easily? Are all works well-lit?
- Is there artist identification (tag, plaque, or business card) with each artwork?
- Are the works—and the gallery—clean? Some clutter, especially around the desk area, is usually expected, but are the frames dust-free and the glass free of finger marks? Does the overall gallery space give the impression that someone cares about the business and the artworks? Do the works appear to be well maintained?
- Are the gallery's sales personnel helpful and knowledgeable? If you ask a question about a work or an artist, does the salesperson share some insight to interest you in the work or the artist? Is there a level of friendliness and expertise which might prompt you to come back to this gallery?
- What is the ambiance of the gallery? What feeling do you get when you first walk through the door? Do you feel welcome or like an intruder? Do you feel comfortable viewing the artworks at your own pace?

Consider your own artwork as you answer the following questions:

- Does the gallery specialize in one particular medium, style, or subject matter? If not, which media, styles, or subjects are most prominent?
- Are you comfortable with the level of professionalism of the artists whose works are shown? Do you find yourself respecting these artists?
- What is the price range of the majority of the works? Can you find out the range of the gallery's best sellers?
- How long has the gallery been in business? What are its business hours? Does it close for any extended period of time (like wintertime for a summer resort gallery)?
- How frequently are works changed?
- How does it promote its artists? Can visitors pick up promotional/informational materials in the gallery? Does it advertise

in newspapers or magazines?
- Does it have one-person or group shows?
- What type of clientele does it cater to? Tourists? Local collectors? Corporations? Interior decorators?
- Does it handle works on consignment or outright purchase? If consignment, what is its commission percentage?

In-person visits are easiest for scouting local galleries, but what about those out of town? These evaluations are important enough to plan a trip, either as a vacation or as a business trip with other artists, to visit galleries within a preplanned area. If this is impossible, select galleries in cities where you have friends or relatives. Ask someone whose judgment you trust to visit the galleries and be your eyes and ears. Send them your list of questions. When you get the list back, understand that some of the answers will be factual and others subjective.

If no relative or friend can evaluate the galleries you want to learn about, telephone the gallery. Most gallery personnel won't have the time to answer all of your questions, but you can elicit the basics, such as whether it specializes, hours of operation, length of time in business, types of artwork it prefers, and name of contact person for artist review. Also request that a gallery brochure or informational piece be sent to you. Staple or paperclip these pieces to your evaluation card so that all information is filed together.

Evaluating a Shop

If shops are your market area, use most of the evaluation questions that are listed for galleries. Instead of looking for a particular style or medium of fine art that the shop specializes in, however, determine if it has a theme or leans toward a particular type of item. Don't expect the personnel to be exceptionally knowledgeable about each artist it carries, and don't be surprised if fine artworks don't always have a card or plaque advertising the artist's name.

As you visit shops for evaluation, bear in mind that some shops not currently exhibiting paintings might be interested if your work is especially appropriate. Perhaps the shop owner simply never thought of handling fine art or believes an artist wouldn't be interested in having his/her work there. Approach the owner with the idea, being open to a trial period on consignment. It could be a great sales opportunity for both of you.

Evaluating a Booth Show

Visit the shows that most interest you and ask yourself:

- How are the booths laid out? What is the pedestrian traffic flow around the booths? Do some participants seem to be out in no-man's land with few shoppers?
- What kind of area is it in? Is there adequate room for people to see the works and browse? Are there any other attractions like food or entertainment to attract shoppers? Is the show located on grass, dirt (which equals dust) or asphalt? In what season was the show held, and was it a wise choice? Is the show the main attraction or simply an aspect of a larger celebration?
- What is the mood of the crowd? Are they having a good time? Hostile? Disappointed? Is it a buying crowd, that is, are people walking around with works under their arms?
- What is the level of professionalism in the exhibited artwork? Can you respect a majority of the works you see? How would your work fit in here?

Next, gather information as a potential artist-exhibitor:

- How long has the show been in existence? The more years a show has been offered, the better the chance that the sponsors are reliable, exhibitors are happy, and sales are at least adequate.
- Who are the sponsors? An individual, group, or professional show exhibitor? Does the sponsor take a commission on your sales? Is the commission in addition to or in lieu of a booth fee?
- What is the booth fee? Is your work screened or prejudged to be accepted for a space? What is the jurying process? Who were the judges? Is there an entry fee?

HOW TO FILL OUT EVALUATION CARDS

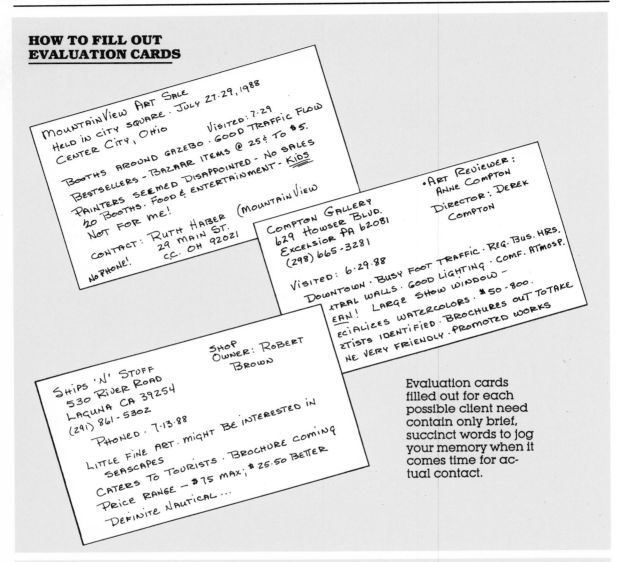

MountainView Art Sale
Held in city square · July 27-29, 1988
Center City, Ohio   Visited: 7.29

Booths around gazebo · Good Traffic Flow
Bestsellers - Bazaar items @ 25¢ to $5.
Painters seemed Disappointed - No sales
20 Booths · Food & Entertainment - Kids
Not for me!

Contact: Ruth Haber (MountainView)
               29 Main St.
               CC. OH 92021
No Phone!

Compton Gallery
629 Howser Blvd.
Excelsior PA 62081
(298) 665-3281

·Art Reviewer:
 Anne Compton
Director: Derek
         Compton

Visited: 6·29·88

Downtown · Busy foot traffic · Reg· Bus. Hrs.
ntral walls · Good lighting · Comf. Atmosp.
ean! Large show window -
ecializes watercolors · $50-800·
rtists identified · Brochures out to take
ne very friendly ·Promoted works

Ships 'N' Stuff
530 River Road
Laguna CA 39254
(291) 861-5302

Shop
Owner: Robert
       Brown

Phoned · 7·13·88
Little fine art · might be interested in
Seascapes
Caters to Tourists · Brochure coming
Price Range - $75 max; $25.50 better
Definite Nautical ...

Evaluation cards filled out for each possible client need contain only brief, succinct words to jog your memory when it comes time for actual contact.

TRY LOCAL GALLERIES FIRST

Ray Friesz, noted Laguna Niguel, California, artist sells through galleries, commissions, and studio shows, and to corporations. He passes this advice along to artists about researching galleries:

"Personally visit galleries within your reach. Note those that handle work somewhat in the direction of yours. Number the galleries according to your preference. Visit them again in order of preference, but not with the pressure of having to show your work. Personally talk to the staff or director, stating admiration of his/her gallery. Let them know you're an artist and not a buyer. They may or may not ask you questions about your work, but don't try to promote it yourself on this visit. If they don't ask you to send slides, then mention as you're leaving that you may like to send them slides or show them your work sometime. Tell them your name. You've 'broken the ice.' "

- How do you get a prospectus? Where and to whom do you write or call? Read every prospectus carefully. This is your list of rules and most shows do not waver regarding them.
- Are any prizes or awards offered? If so, who were the jurors? Are the awards/ prizes for individual works or booth display? When is the award jurying done?

Ask participating artists:

- What are their feelings about the show overall? Were the sponsors helpful or hostile? Were any display materials provided free or were they rentable?
- Have any artists done this show before? If so, why did they come back?

Evaluating a Juried Competition

It's difficult to evaluate a juried competition because ordinarily you don't view the exhibition, talk to the other artists, or meet the judges.

You'll have to rely heavily on the prospectus that the competition sponsors send out. Read the prospectus carefully and evaluate:

- The number of times this competition has been held.
- The reputation of its sponsor.
- The reputations of the entry judges and the awards judges.
- Conditions attached to acceptance into the show and to award winners.
- Clarity of entry deadline, entry qualifications, delivery of accepted pieces, acceptable shipping methods, date of award judging and announcement, pick-up dates.
- Types of awards, number of awards, amounts of cash prizes, exhibitions, and catalogs.
- Fees over and above an entry fee. If it seems to you that you are "paying" to be in the show, avoid the competition. However, it is not uncommon to assume responsibility for shipping to and from the show.

Consider entering the competition if the competition prospectus clearly outlines this pertinent information, if it's offering a reputable sponsor and judges, has been held before, and seems fair to you in its rules and fees. If you enter, maintain solid notes about any difficulty encountered, whether rejected or accepted. Competition information, especially names and addresses, will change from year to year, but you'll ascertain what you did and didn't like about a particular competition through your cards.

If the competition's prospectus is vague about the identity of the judges or the sponsor, when the awards will be given, exhibition of accepted pieces, exact awards or prize money, or when accepted works will be returned to artists, either avoid the competition or phone for further information. Occasionally prospectuses are mailed before final details are ironed out; a phone call can give you the facts. But vague prospectuses can also mean a lack of organization on the sponsor's part (which spells disaster), or a mediocre competition which you don't want to enter.

Prospectuses can also lie—judges may be listed who haven't even been contacted; prize money, though promised, hasn't been raised. Unfortunately, there's no way to discern this just from reading a prospectus. Disreputable competitions, thankfully, often have a short lifespan as misappropriated judges object to the use of their names and winning artists who have not been paid make the fact public. Networking with other artists and art organizations and reading art publications help to keep you informed about which competitions are honest.

Adapt any of these questions to the other outlets not specifically covered here and maintain the information on your evaluation cards.

You now have a stack of cards on the specific outlets you're definitely going to contact. All the client information you need is at your fingertips.

SELF-PROMOTION

Self-promotion and marketing are two sides of the same coin and are difficult to separate much of the time. But self-promotion—the ongoing process of building name recognition and a reputation—isn't necessarily tied into the actual marketing of your work. In self-promotion, you're identifying and establishing yourself as an artist, not only to potential clients, but to the community as well. You're letting everyone, regardless of potential art-buying possibilities, know who you are and what you do. You're blowing your own horn whenever and wherever you tactfully can do so.

Selling art is a people business. The more people you know, the more people you talk to, the greater your chance of making a sale. Relatives, friends, and neighbors all have other contacts. If *your* contacts don't know you're an artist and the type of work you do, they can't tell *their* contacts. Many business contacts begin as social ones, so always carry your business card with you. Don't be afraid in a social setting to say who you are and what you do. Get the word around.

Self-promotional efforts should be well planned, but not necessarily as refined and strategic as marketing efforts. Generally, you're attempting to let everyone know of your skill and talent, not just people likely to buy your work.

Local Self-promotion

Local self-promotion is accomplished through volunteering, organization membership, social contacts, press releases, and staged events.

Volunteering time and talent increases your community visibility. Be willing to do "free-bies," to donate your work, time, and talent. Libraries, hospitals, and philanthropic organizations often need help in organizing charity art auctions, exhibitions, and sales, or need artwork to sell at these events. The people involved with these institutions and organizations are also people who can do *you* the most good. They are frequently upwardly mobile, and, as well as being interested in art, they can afford to buy it.

Join artists' associations, both national and local. Local associations often provide emotional and moral support, information on shows and competitions, inside information on area galleries, opportunity to learn through classes, and a network with other artists.

Some also offer a membership gallery, a newsletter to keep you abreast of business and legislative measures affecting artists, and even discounts at local art supply stores.

National organizations put you in touch with the community of artists nationwide. Your membership fees help to provide: lobbyists for federal legislation favoring artists; newsletters which inform you about national happenings, hazardous materials, and the status of artists; the ability to take advantage of group insurance rates; and access to tax, copyright, and contractual information. Your participation in both the local and national organizations gives you visibility and name recognition as well as credibility as an artist who cares about the advancement of art and artists' rights.

Offer to give free lectures or to teach classes. The local Boy Scout troop might not sound like the place to drum up business, but Boy Scouts have parents, and enthusiastic endorsements from their youngsters stick in parents' minds. Local colleges, universities, and high schools offer night classes. Even if no concrete sales arise, you profit by gaining the reputation as the local watercolor (or oil, or acrylics) "expert." Publicity through the school's class brochure doesn't hurt, either. Present demonstrations at senior citizen centers, art supply stores, malls, special interest groups—an artist demonstrating an art medium and technique is a strong "drawing" card.

Join business organizations. As an independent fine artist you're operating as a self-employed businessperson. You not only learn information about how to run your personal business better, but develop information on the new businesses opening in town, new construction, and future planned developments. These lead to areas where your work can be hung or purchased. You also meet company presidents and executives who can be potential buyers.

Advertise and/or participate in local and state literature published by tourist departments to promote the arts and crafts in a state. Contact your state's tourism department (located in the state's capital city) and city tourist/visitor bureau to find out the requirements for inclusion in any art-related publication they offer. Some areas also offer publications that are privately produced which inform people about the area's artists. When you hear about or see one of these publications, contact the publisher for details regarding inclusion.

Send press releases and photographs to your local newspapers and art publications every time an event occurs related to your artwork. This might be an award, participation in a charitable event, a lecture/demonstration, an exhibition, an opening—any newsworthy item that ties in with your art career. Keep press releases to one page, if possible. The first paragraph should focus on the primary event and answer the who, what, where, when, and why. Explanatory facts filling in details come next, and biographical information should be last. A photograph of the event, you, or the artwork involved should accompany the release.

HOW TO USE YOUR REPRINTS

"Kingfishers and Lotus" Watercolor 20" x 60"

BEVERLY JUNE STEWART

Traditional Oriental brush watercolor

Represented in Albuquerque by Concetta D. Fine Art, El Dor Gallery, Weems Winrock Gallery
STUDIO: 1133 MARIGOLD DR NE, ALBQ, NM 87122   505/294-8177

Beverly Stewart's full color card is reprinted from a regional gallery guide she advertised in, titled *The Collector's Guide*, published by Pamela and Don Michaelis. This particular guide offers a host of information— gallery/studio and museum overviews and indexes, maps, directories, an event and exhibition calendar, and more. It's a boon to anyone, native or visitor, to find artwork suited to each taste, and is distributed to public areas, such as motels and hotels. Stewart uses this reprint as a business card in addition to her black-and-white card (see page 63) because it shows an example of her work.

CHAPTER THREE
CHECKLISTS

Goals of any marketing effort are:
- [ ] To inform public of product's existence
- [ ] To show how product meets public's needs and desires
- [ ] To inform public where and how product can be purchased

Use these six marketing steps to reach your marketing goals:
- [ ] Analyze your product
- [ ] Determine your target markets
- [ ] Locate clients within your target markets
- [ ] Develop your marketing strategy and tools
- [ ] Initiate a marketing plan
- [ ] Evaluate and update your marketing efforts periodically

Use these resources to locate clients:
- [ ] Yellow Pages
- [ ] Business and city directories
- [ ] Newspapers
- [ ] Art magazines
- [ ] Trade magazines
- [ ] Reference books
- [ ] Libraries
- [ ] State art councils
- [ ] Tourist or visitor bureaus
- [ ] Other artists
- [ ] Association newsletters
- [ ] Chambers of commerce
- [ ] Business organizations

To develop an effective client list:
- [ ] Research each name and address
- [ ] Evaluate each for suitability to your work

- [ ] Use friends and relatives, if possible, for in-person visit to out-of-town outlets
- [ ] Record information on 3″ × 5″ index card
- [ ] Always obtain the name of a contact person

To evaluate a gallery or shop, check the following points:
- [ ] Environment of the gallery building
- [ ] How artwork is displayed
- [ ] If artists are identified with their artwork
- [ ] Expertise and helpfulness of the gallery's personnel
- [ ] What medium, style, or subject matter the gallery specializes in
- [ ] Level of artists' professionalism
- [ ] Price range of works
- [ ] Price range of best-sellers
- [ ] Business history
- [ ] Business hours
- [ ] Advertising and promotion policy
- [ ] Exhibition policy
- [ ] Type of clientele
- [ ] Method of handling artworks, whether work is consigned or purchased

When evaluating a booth show, check for:
- [ ] Layout of booths
- [ ] Pedestrian traffic flow
- [ ] Environment of the show
- [ ] Length of the show
- [ ] Level of professionalism of exhibited works

☐ History of the show
☐ Reputation of sponsor
☐ Amount of booth fee
☐ Size of booth space
☐ If there is a sponsor commission
☐ Entry requirements
☐ Availability of awards
☐ Opinions of participating artists
☐ Helpfulness of sponsors
☐ Availability of display apparatus

Points to consider when evaluating a
juried art competition:
☐ Number of times competition held
☐ Sponsor's reputation
☐ Reputation of entry judges and
   awards judges
☐ Conditions attached to acceptance
☐ Conditions attached to awards
☐ Deadlines
☐ Shipping methods permitted
☐ Type and number of awards
☐ Additional rewards, such as exhibi-
   tion and catalog inclusion
☐ Additional fees above entry fee

CHAPTER 4
TOOLS OF THE TRADE

The three marketing steps covered in the previous chapter have armed you with the pertinent information you need to begin the active marketing process. You know the product (you and your work), you've found target market areas, and you have a researched list of clients you're going to contact.

Now you're ready for step four — developing your marketing strategy and tools.

To begin your strategy planning, make these decisions:

- Am I contacting my clients in person, through the mail, or both?
- How much money have I allocated to my marketing and promotion campaign?
- Am I budgeting my money so that my marketing and self-promotion endeavors are a continuing effort?

These decisions are important because they dictate the type and order of development of your marketing tools.

Your method of contact is important because a client list of primarily in-person reviews means directing great attention to a quality review portfolio and printed marketing materials suitable for a leave-behind packet. Mailed submissions necessitate producing three to five quality samples, but special attention must be given to printed materials that create the greatest impact and communicate the most information about you and your work without benefit of your physical presence. If you are planning both types of contact, then a great deal of thought must be given to samples and printed materials that are effective in both situations.

The amount of money you've allocated for marketing influences the number and type of samples you obtain as well as the quality and combination of printed materials you select. Allocate the most money to the best samples possible. As you create individual printed pieces, evaluate the unit they create as a whole. When combined, they should present to the client:

- Excellent examples of your work.
- Your name, address, and phone number.
- Background information on your art-related career.
- Your skills, medium, and subject matter directed to the client's specific area of interest.

Budgeting your money is essential because you need to plan for mailers or flyers as follow-up and reminder mailings. Printing follow-up materials simultaneously with your original materials assures the same paper and ink colors. Sometimes (depending on the pieces, your printer, and press/paper capabilities) printing in quantity and printing several pieces on a single press run are money-saving devices.

Other points to keep in mind while developing your marketing materials are:

- Understand your needs. Evaluate the purpose of each marketing tool, analyze what it can and can't do for you at this time, and plan it to work hand-in-hand with other tools to create a strong, visually coordinated unit.
- Know the type of presentation your market demands. Your market research should convey to you the competitive level you're encountering. If you're aiming for only top-of-the-line, high-prestige galleries in New York or Los Angeles, for example, be prepared to invest in a professionally designed marketing package and top-notch transparencies. These galleries are being approached by professional artists nationwide and the competition is keen.

Focus your materials to your potential clients' interests. For example, if you're approaching galleries, these directors are most interested in other galleries where your work has been handled, shows/exhibits you've had, awards you've won, and so on. If approaching greeting card publishers, you should inform them about other publishers who have printed your cards or, in lieu of that experience, any instance when your work has appeared in printed form, because their main interest is how well your work will reproduce in print. Be sure your own printed marketing tools sparkle with accurate reproduction to bring home this point.

Develop multi-purpose printed marketing tools, especially if money is tight. Use letter-head designed for cover letters for your resume, bills of sale, contracts, information sheets, and general correspondence. The heavy paper flyer showing six examples of your work and an awards list slips easily into a mailing package or leave-behind packet. It can also be folded and sent out as a self-mailer reminder to clients who haven't seen those works before.

Realize that no single printed piece meets all of your communication needs. You can't write

These are slide sheets—the plastic sheets designed to hold up to twenty slides. Always choose an archival-quality sheet for the greatest, best-lasting protection. Here one is shown empty, one full of slides ready for labeling, and another cut down, holding only a few slides. These sheets are easily included in a mailing package or in a portfolio. They keep your slides clean, in order, and readily viewable on a light table without removing them from their protective covering.

a cover letter on a brochure or hand out a flyer at a party in place of a business card. Your printed materials work together. If finances are very limited, you might not develop a brochure at all, but choose instead to let several less-expensive pieces do its work.

With these points in mind, let's examine in detail each of the marketing tools available to you.

We'll begin with the most important communicator of your artistic style, technique, medium, and subject matter—your art samples.

TYPES OF SAMPLES

Samples fall into two broad categories: reproductions and original works. Their purpose is to show what you do, how well you do it, and the depth of your skill and talent.

There are five types of samples:

- Slides/transparencies.
- Photographs.
- Photostats.
- Photocopies.
- Original works.

The first four are reproductions of your work; the fifth, in this context, refers to original paintings, drawings, one-of-a-kind prints, and tearsheets—final printed products, such as greeting cards.

Slides and Transparencies

This is the sample type selected by most fine artists because it's the one most frequently requested for review and jurying. Slides and transparencies are the same; a transparency is a *positive* film image (as opposed to the negative image for photographic prints) that varies in size according to film size. A slide is a transparency mounted in a sturdy frame, commonly called a slide "mount." The most useful transparency size for art samples is made with 35mm film and called 35mm slides.

Slides are small, light, easy to handle, relatively inexpensive, and good communicators of color, subject matter, and medium. Competitions and booth shows most frequently request this type of sample.

The greatest disadvantage to slides is that

you need some kind of viewing apparatus to perceive the full impact of your work. A slide projector allows your work to be "blown up" and seen at its best advantage. Many competition judges and booth show jurors utilize projectors; some galleries are equipped with projection facilities. Other apparatus used for slide viewing are somewhat less desirable; these include hand-held viewers, light tables, loupes, and overhead lights.

Some models of hand-held viewers provide modest magnification; others merely illuminate the slide from behind. Invest in a viewer with both capabilities. If you take slides to an in-person review, be prepared with a viewer in case the client has only a light table available or the projector is broken. A viewer is also valuable for reviewing and editing slides at home.

A light table (a table or moveable box with a clear top and a light source shining through it from below) doesn't magnify your slides; they can be viewed, but detail and impact are lost.

A loupe is simply a magnifying eye piece. It helps to "enlarge" detail, but isn't as good as a viewer.

Then there is the "hold-them-up-to-the-light" approach. This does the least to reveal anything good about your work, but everyone does it at some time and gallery directors and jurors are no exception. Because you can never be sure how your slides will be viewed, each slide must be the best.

A good slide possesses these qualities:

■ It's color-true—the slide's reproduced color matches the color in the original work.

■ The photographed work fills the film frame, the image area of the slide. If the artwork is not proportional to the slide's image area, it should be centered with equal amounts of space top and bottom and even amounts of space on each side.

■ No distracting articles or printed background fabrics are in the frame. These draw attention away from the work. "Sweeps," large rolls of neutral or black background paper, are available at most photography and some art supply stores. They provide a clean background and are easily re-rolled and stored until the next use. Velvet, velour or velveteen cloth are nonreflective, but select a color most appropriate to your work. The work should stand out from the background. Photograph dark subjects on a background matched to a neutral value within the artwork.

■ The edges of the photographed work are straight and centered. If the artwork appears to be narrower at the top or bottom, or one side seems shorter than the other, the camera wasn't parallel to the artwork when it was photographed. These works should be rephotographed. If a work is photographed off-center, special opaque photographic masking tape (available at photography stores) can be applied to the slide to reduce unwanted background areas so that only the desired image is projected. But it's time-consuming to mask each slide and is unsightly in a slide sheet; you're wiser to photograph the work properly in the beginning.

■ The photographed work is in focus and sharp.

■ The proper lighting has been used to avoid glare or "hot spots."

Always duplicate slides; make them yourself or have a photography lab do it. They're necessary for your portfolio, multiple slide submissions, and to keep a studio record of your work. If you're doing your own photography and feel comfortable with your skills, duplicate slides can be made by shooting the same piece of artwork over and over again as many times as you need slides. These "duplicates" supply greater clarity and are more color-true than lab-produced duplicates, because each slide is actually an "original" shot. However, if a mistake is made on the first shot, that error is repeated on each slide.

If a photography lab is making your dupes, the lab takes your one "original" slide and, in essence, rephotographs it using special slide film, lights, and so on. Because of this, there can be a loss of sharpness, an increase in contrast, and possibly a slight shift in color balance. No duplicate made in this manner is as good as the original, but the better the lab, the closer the match. Therefore, you want to find the *best* lab.

Present your slides to potential clients in

slide sheets, clear plastic sheets containing up to 20 individual pockets, one slide to each pocket. Always choose an archival-quality slide sheet. Most have holes for storage in a three-ring binder or portfolio. If you're mailing or leaving behind only a few slides, cut the slide sheet to accommodate the number of slides.

Photographs

Photographs can be a very important sample choice, either used alone or in conjunction with slides. If you don't anticipate needing slides for competitions or booth show jurying, then consider photographs of your work to use in your portfolio, to send in mailing packages, or to glue onto specially designed printed marketing tools.

If your artwork is in color, then definitely choose color photography; if you work in black and white, then you can choose between color or black and white. The preferred size is 8"x10", though 5"x7" or 4"x6" is acceptable.

Advantages to photographs are:

- Once the work is shot, the photographic print can be printed larger or smaller to fit a particular need.
- They are light and relatively inexpensive.
- A special apparatus isn't needed for viewing.
- Once you own a negative, numerous duplicate prints can be made with little degradation of the image.
- There is latitude in the darkroom to print only the part of the negative that's considered desirable, compensating for errors that occurred during the photography session.
- For black-and-white photographs, you can request a contact sheet and review the printed negatives before deciding which you want enlarged and printed.

There are some disadvantages to photographs. They never have quite the visual impact of a projected slide, they require greater storage space, and they can bend, tear, and fade if not cared for properly.

A good photograph fills the same requirements as a good slide (see page 47).

When having photographic prints made from your negatives, go to a professional photography lab rather than the photo finisher who processes snapshots. You want your photographs to receive specialized attention.

Photographs can be stored in the boxes you receive from the photo lab when you pick them up or in any appropriately sized box that keeps them from sliding and bending. Acetate or vinyl "sleeves" protect photographs in portfolios and mailing packages. Acetate is cheaper but scratches easily. Both types of sleeves are available with holes to accommodate three-ring or "toothed" binders and can be purchased at art supply, photography, office supply, and many stationery stores.

Whether you select photographs or slides as samples, keep at least one copy in a file in your studio. This personal studio portfolio is an invaluable record of your work in case a call comes from a previous client who wants a painting similar to "the one you did for my aunt" or from a writer who wants to do a story on you and needs accompanying examples. There may not be time to photograph everything, but make an effort to have your most successful pieces reproduced.

Photostats

Photostatting is an inexpensive photographic process that creates a high-contrast, deep black image on brilliant white paper. Consider it for samples only if you create black-and-white line work. A special photostatic camera prints on lightweight photographic paper directly as a positive; no negative is involved. Photostats are recommended primarily as nonreturnable samples in mailing packages and leave-behinds, but they can also be used in portfolios. Consider them especially if you anticipate approaching graphic art fields with your pen-and-ink artwork.

Advantages to photostats as samples are:

- Work can be enlarged and reduced in size. Odd-size work can be reproduced on same-size sheets providing uniformity within a portfolio or mailing package.
- Corrections can be made to the original work. Type-correction fluid or white tem-

pera is ideal for small corrections; white paper blocks entire sections of actual artwork or a tearsheet.

- They are less expensive than slides and photographs (including photography expenses).
- Numerous reproductions are possible.
- They produce a clear, crisp reproduction.

On the minus side, photostats are not appropriate for color. They do not offer as "slick" a presentation as do slides, and they bend and tear if not protected.

The care and protection of photostats is the same as for photographs (see page 48).

Photostatting services are available in most cities and are listed in the Yellow Pages and business directories. Work with the photostat cameraperson by giving clear verbal or written instructions to obtain the best photostats possible. Listen to any advice regarding how well your work will reproduce.

Photocopies

A photocopy is the least expensive of reproductions made by photographic means. Photocopiers are available to the public in the library, business office, drugstore, and copying centers. These machines produce a direct positive image on nonphotographic paper. Like photostats, they should be considered only for black-and-white artwork. Photocopies are not recommended for the portfolio but can be used as nonreturnable mailed and leave-behind samples.

Advantages to photocopies are:

- Work can be enlarged and reduced in size—odd-size work can be reproduced on same-size sheets providing uniformity within a portfolio or mailing package.
- Reproduction cost is minimal.
- Numerous reproductions are possible.
- They are the least expensive reproductions.
- They are usable as nonreturnable samples.
- A variety of papers and lightweight cardboards can be used since the process isn't restricted to photographic papers.

Photocopiers vary in quality of reproduction. Copies must be free of dots, smudges, and extraneous lines. Color photocopying is available, but the ability to match a wide range of colors is still limited and "muddy" reproductions can result. Talk with the person operating the machine for advice on the quality of reproduction you'll receive for your type of work. Color photocopies are more expensive than black and white.

Some size restrictions apply. Many machines cannot handle work larger than 11"x17". Enlargement and reduction capabilities vary by machine.

Photocopies don't possess the "snap" of photostats, and don't present as professional-looking a package. They bend, wrinkle, and tear easily.

Care and protection of photocopies is the same as for photographs (see page 48).

Photocopying services are listed in the Yellow Pages and business directories. When selecting a service, explain your use for these reproductions to the photocopier operator and request that special attention be given to the copies. Inquire about paper selection; heavier stock paper or lightweight cardboard increases the professional appearance of the samples.

Original Work

Original artwork is the most communicative of sample types since it allows the potential client to see firsthand your style, medium, use of color, subject matter and artistic ability. The disadvantages are that it's difficult to transport, it's not appropriate for mailing packages, and, if lost, is impossible to replace.

If showing original work at a gallery/shop review, unframed works must be protected from handling. If your work is on paper, insert the painting between two pieces of matboard, a solid back and a frontal mat "frame." For maximum protection, wrap the entire article in acetate. If you want the painting to be more "viewable," lightly attach the painting to the solid back matboard with double stick tape and frame it with matting; glue the matting lightly around the edges, being very careful not to get glue near or on the painting. This gives the client something to hold onto without interfering with the view of the actual painting. For further protection, place a sheet of clear acetate between the artwork and the outside mat frame and glue the three segments together. If a gallery director elbows a cup of coffee over your artwork, the matting is stained, but the artwork beneath the acetate should remain coffee-free.

Unframed canvas works are at the greatest risk for damage. Transport them with caution so that the unprotected fronts are not gouged or scratched. If you show them at an in-person review, hope the reviewer knows better than to simply grab at the painting. If there's any doubt in your mind, give gentle instructions or show by personal example, handling only the flat edges or gently holding the stretcher bars.

Tearsheets

Tearsheets are examples of your work in printed form as final products. The magazine page containing your editorial illustration, a mechanically reproduced print, or the greeting card you illustrated—all are examples of tearsheets.

Use tearsheets when the market area you're approaching needs to see how your work appears when printed. Most times these are the graphic art market areas.

Tearsheets easily become torn and fingermarked. They yellow with age, are difficult to present easily in a portfolio (especially if different sizes and types), and can be hard to obtain if your client doesn't supply them.

If you have only a single printed copy of your work, the challenge is to keep it clean and intact, yet still usable as a sample. Several options are:

- Protect it with a plastic cover in your portfolio.
- Photograph it and use slides or prints as samples while the original stays safely in your studio.
- Mount it on a piece of matboard so that, when showing it at an in-person review, the client handles the matboard, not the piece.
- Laminate it after photographing it.
- Ask the graphic art client's permission to reprint it at your cost so that you have multiple samples.

If you own multiple tearsheets of the printed piece, simply replace it with a clean sample when the old one becomes soiled or torn from handling. For mailed submissions, send an actual tearsheet only if you own numerous copies; otherwise send a photographic print or slide of the tearsheet.

HOW TO LABEL YOUR SAMPLES

All samples should be labeled; samples destined for mailing packages or a client's file *must* be labeled. Labeling immediately identifies a piece should it become separated from the rest of your materials and it supplies pertinent information regarding the artwork. If submitting samples to a competition or booth show, follow the labeling procedures requested in the prospectus. Otherwise follow the instructions outlined as follows:

To Label Slides: On the front of the slide mount (work is correctly oriented as you look at it), print the title of the artwork, medium, actual size of the artwork, year date of comple-

HOW TO LABEL SLIDES

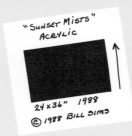

This typical slide has been labeled by utilizing white self-adhesive labels cut into strips. Labeling puts all your pertinent information at the client's fingertips, orients the slide, and indicates ownership should the slide be separated from your other materials. The slide on the left shows the "front"; on the right, the "back."

tion, your copyright notice (a C with a circle around it, the year of completion or publication, and your name), and an arrow indicating the correct orientation of the original work (arrow should point to the top). A reference number may correlate to an information sheet. The back of the slide contains your name, address, and phone number, including area code.

Some of the labor can be taken out of this process if your have your name, address, and phone number put on a rubber stamp made specifically to fit the slide mount. Another stamp can contain your copyright notice without the year date. If the slide mounts are plastic and resist ink, use white self-adhesive labels cut to fit the slides. These are available in discount and stationery stores.

To Label Photographs: All photographs should be labeled with the same important information recommended for slides. Label only the back of the photograph and don't write directly on it, because disfiguring marks will show through to the front. Buy white, self-adhesive labels and type or print your information there.

Two or more labels are often necessary. Type all repetitive information, such as your name and address, at one sitting or buy a rubber stamp and stamp your labels. Or, have self-adhesive labels printed with your name, address, and logo for even more convenience, visibility, and unification of your marketing "package."

Photostats and photocopies, especially those to be retained in a client's files or included in a mailing package, should be labeled in the same manner as photographs.

Original works, if they are works matted specifically for use in your portfolio for an in-person review, should be labeled on the back in the same manner as for photographs. Because of the heavier quality of the matboard, a business card can be glued to the back to save time.

Tearsheets are difficult to label. If only one side needs to be seen by a reviewer, attach self-adhesive labels containing your pertinent information to the back of its protective cover. If it needs to be seen from both sides, place a

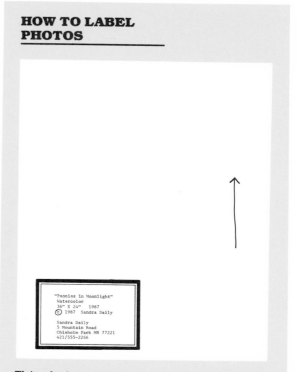

HOW TO LABEL PHOTOS

"Peonies in Moonlight"
Watercolor
36" X 24"   1987
© 1987 Sandra Daily

Sandra Daily
5 Mountain Road
Chisholm Park MN 77221
421/555-2266

This photograph was quickly labeled by using a red-bordered report-cover label available at drug and discount stores. The artwork's pertinent information is easily seen by the client and you're identified should the photo become separated. A plain white self-adhesive label holds the orientation arrow.

small self-adhesive dot bearing an information sheet reference number on its protective clear cover. Correlate the number to an accompanying information sheet.

PHOTOGRAPHING ARTWORK

Search for a photographer experienced in shooting two-dimensional artwork and who understands the importance of this copy of your artwork. Ask to see previous work or request the names of other artists for whom the photographer has worked.

Discuss fees before any shooting begins. Some photographers charge a flat fee, some an hourly fee. Ask if there is an extra charge for developing and printing. In some cases it's less expensive for you to take the undeveloped film to a professional film lab.

Decide if you want both color and black-and-white photography. Even if you work in color, at times it's advantageous to have black-and-white prints for publication. It's easier for the photographer to shoot both color and black and white at one time, saving a second trip.

Negotiate to own all of the negatives, prints, and slides. You want this clearly understood (preferably in writing) before any work is begun.

Understand the photographer's policy if you're dissatisfied with the final product. Some will reshoot the works at no cost; others charge half price; still others require full price.

Photographing Your Own Works

Always photograph your work indoors to insure complete control of the lighting.

You'll need the following equipment to do your own photography:

- A 35mm single lens reflex (SLR) camera with a manual exposure system and an exposure meter or manual override on an automatic exposure system; independent control of the lens aperture and shutter speed; and a 50mm lens, suitable for photographing most works. To photograph small pieces, you'll need a macro lens or close-up attachment to get the camera close enough to fill the entire frame with the piece in sharp focus.
- A cable release.
- A sturdy tripod.
- Film.
- Two floodlights.
- Floodlight reflectors and stands.
- A Kodak Gray Card and color scale.
- Neutral sweeps or background.
- A correcting filter (if needed).
- A diffusion screen or photographic umbrella for each floodlight to control reflections, if the work you're photographing is glossy.

Owning all your equipment requires a substantial financial investment, but if you photograph your work consistently, the investment will be worthwhile in the long run. To reduce this initial investment, investigate used equipment, either through a reputable camera store or photography magazines (*Shutterbug*, *Popular Photography*, *Modern Photography*, for example). If you're merely experimenting with photography, initially rent or borrow the equipment.

The film you use depends on the type of sample you desire. For color slides, use Kodak Ektachrome 50 Prof with an ASA of 50; for color prints, use Kodacolor VR-G 100 with an ASA of 100, and for black-and-white prints, choose Plus-X Pan with an ASA of 125.

SHOOTING THE WORKS

California artist Susan Greaves knows the importance of quality slides when entering competitions. She photographs her own works. According to Greaves, "Once I got the right set-up of lights, and the film and lights balanced, I started to get into a lot more shows."

When asked if it took her a long time to learn how to photograph her work, her response was a quick "no." She read articles on how to do it in *American Artist* and in *The Artist's Magazine*. "They spelled out the specific type of lightbulb, film, everything. I didn't even try to understand it—I just took it to a camera shop and said this is what I need and the salesman gave it to me. I came home and started shooting and it works beautifully. All you need is a 35mm camera and two lights and a piece of black fabric to hang behind your work and that's it. It's not that complicated once you understand the steps."

Buy two 3200-degree Kelvin bulbs for your floodlights; if you're using Kodacolor VR-G 100, you also need an 80A color compensating filter for the camera with this light source. Check with the photography store personnel for other options and best combination of film, filters, and floodlights for your specific needs.

If your artwork is framed beneath glass, remove it, if at all possible, to avoid glare. Hang supported work on a neutral blank wall, place it on an easel or shelf, or rest it on the floor and lean it against the wall. A sweep or neutral fabric/paper behind it provides a nonreflective background. You can attach unsupported paper works to the wall or background with low-tack adhesive or double-stick tape.

Secure your camera to the tripod and attach the cable release so you can trip the shutter without shaking the camera. Check the camera for height and parallel alignment to the work. Move the camera until the piece fills the frame in sharp focus.

Arrange the floodlights, one on each side, at 45-degree angles to the piece until flat, even illumination is achieved. One way to check for even illumination is to hold a piece of white paper against the piece being photographed. A pencil held in front of the paper should cast shadows of equal density if your lighting is even. Uneven illumination causes one side of the piece to be darker than the other; adjust the lights to avoid this problem.

Use the Kodak Gray Card and color scale to determine the correct exposure; taking a light meter reading directly from the artwork can result in an inaccurate exposure. Place the card in front of the piece to be photographed. Set the f-stop to f/8 and determine the proper shutter speed. Be sure you have the correct ASA set on your camera for the type of film you're using. Set this shutter speed on your camera. Recheck your focus and alignment, and take the picture using your cable release.

For insurance, repeat the process at the same shutter speed, but "bracket" your exposures. This means taking one picture one f-stop above and another picture one f-stop below your original setting. In this case, you would use f/11 and f/5.6 for the next two exposures. Record your shots in a notebook. Repeat this process for each piece. When your slides or prints are returned, they'll be in the order you shot them. Refer to your data sheet to learn which setting provides the best reproduction of your work.

More useful information on art photography can be found in *Photographing Your Artwork*, by Russell Hart.

DEVELOPING A PORTFOLIO

If in-person reviews are part of your marketing strategy, you'll own at least one portfolio, possibly two. A portfolio is simply a case that holds your samples and printed marketing tools. No hard and fast rule mandates the "proper" portfolio style. Manufacturers now produce portfolios in a variety of colors and materials and, if your portfolio is small, you might consider a handleless style, although most have two handles for ease of carrying. Some artists, especially those whose works are too large for a standard portfolio, design and custom-make their own cases.

The type and size of the portfolio you buy depends on the samples you're presenting. If you take original artwork to a review, you'll need a portfolio as large as your largest work. Bear in mind, however, that you want to carry it without awkwardness and to show the works comfortably. If the portfolio case is larger than 18"x24", it probably won't fit the reviewer's desk and will have to be leaned against a wall or placed on the floor, forcing you to hand works to the reviewer.

Place original works inside the portfolio in a pre-planned order, organized by subject matter or medium. This not only presents a logical flow of continuity but also allows you to know the exact location of a particular painting if the reviewer makes a specific request. If your works are framed in matboard, all matboard should be the same size, or nearly so — the reviewer's eye picks up a sense of orderliness and unification, the works are easier to handle, and a small work isn't "lost" between two larger works.

The other portfolio you'll need, or the only one if you're not taking original work to the review, is the portfolio containing your reproduction samples — slides or photographs or, in some cases, photostats.

This portfolio should be like a book, with the reviewer turning it page by page. You definitely want it to fit on the reviewer's desk, so choose either a 8½"x11" or 11"x14" case. Many standard cases have pockets for loose pieces or leave-behinds and are available in three-ring or toothed (twenty-eight-ring) binder styles, or without a binder spine. When selecting a case, consider your finances, the size of your samples, and professional appearance. If your finances are rather slim, consider simply buying a top-of-the-line notebook cover.

SHOWING YOUR PORTFOLIO

This sample page of a photograph prepared for a client's viewing illustrates how even a simple notebook cover and protective plastic sheets can make a review professional, easy, and informative. The painting's photograph is accompanied by an information card on its opposite page so the client can read specifics while viewing the artwork. Pages like this can also be placed in your ringspine portfolio case. (Painting by Eleanora Davis.)

HOW TO USE YOUR LOGO

Shirley Gruen of Port Washington, Wisconsin, selected a portion of a mosiac she created from glass pieces found on the beach as the logo for her marketing materials. The mosaic fittingly communicated the openness and freedom of her art and her attachment to the water, formed through her waterfront studio and gallery. The logo is printed in blue with her name, address, and phone in black. She's carried the logo through all of her materials including a two-color brochure, which she uses as a mailer and as a gallery handout, and a self-adhesive label, which customizes all of her envelopes.

This portfolio is the chief communicator for all of the original works you aren't presenting in person. It holds samples of fifteen to twenty works, either slides, photographs, photostats, or all three, arranged in a logical order. Group works by medium or subject matter and direct the samples to the client's interests. A portfolio isn't static; before attending a review, go through it and select the most appropriate works. Your client evaluation cards give you the information you need to edit your portfolio correctly.

Slides should be in slide sheets, and photographs and photostats in acetate or plastic covers. Ring-spine portfolios keep the sample pages in order and allow easy turning. Slides can be accompanied by an information sheet placed at the front of the portfolio or handed to the reviewer. (See pages 69 and 73 for further details on the information sheet.) With ring-spine cases, insert photographs so that the photograph is on the left and an information card centered inside a clear sheet is on the right; or information can be placed on an information sheet, as with slides.

Use dividers to separate the portfolio sections to guide the reviewer through it. You don't want to distract the reviewer with conversation, so arrange the portfolio to speak for itself. Press-on type turns an ordinary three-ring divider into an announcement of what comes next: for example, Florals - Oils; Life Studies; Rural Landscapes in Watercolor. Be as creative as you can—this portfolio represents you and your work—but don't diminish the work inside with extra flourishes or garish colors. If possible, tie the dividers' design to your other business materials through type selection, logo, or graphic elements. It adds to professional appearance and visual unification of your marketing package.

For more creative ideas and information on portfolios, read *How to Prepare Your Portfolio*, by Ed Marquand.

PRINTED MARKETING TOOLS

These materials function as companions to your samples. Each fills a particular role, either alone or in conjunction with other pieces.

As you read through these descriptions,

keep in mind that you need not develop all these materials at once. But establishing design continuity at the outset ultimately results in a visually united package.

If you plan to use a logo, now is the time to plan and design it. It can be a graphic element, typographic device, specially created illustration, or an actual example of your work. Carry this logo throughout your promotional tools.

The Brochure

A brochure is a pamphlet, booklet, or multifold printed piece. It usually presents several examples of your work, personal background information, and career history; at times, it presents a personal statement. Its contents may apply to only one market area, narrowing its usage; if it provides an overview of your skills you can use it with other, more focused pieces to approach specific markets.

A brochure offers several advantages:

- The amount of space gives you freedom to create the very best image of yourself and your work.
- It can be utilized at in-person reviews and in mailed submissions.
- It can stand by itself or work in conjunction with other materials.
- It can be a self-mailer.
- It can be used as a handout at shows/exhibitions.
- It can be available at sales outlets to inform the public about you and your work when you're not there.

The brochure's greatest disadvantage is cost. The same space that allows the inclusion of numerous examples also creates high reproduction and paper expense. You should have firm goals for the brochure in mind so no space is wasted, and you should plan your design to coordinate visually with other materials to increase its usefulness. In addition, you can reduce your brochure's cost by using black-and-white reproduction rather than full color.

The design is limited only by your imagination, but, because a brochure can meet a multitude of needs, think through its intended uses before you begin. Some brochures take the place of resumes by including education, pro-

DESIGNING A BROCHURE

The art of Christopher Bull evokes an intuitive response to a very personal type of imagery. His images are of space: the great, deep space of landscapes, and solitary, private space. His images celebrate light, both as it delineates and defines form, and as it softens and obscures it. Most of all, Christopher's images are about people: reflections of simple, peaceful moments, subtle expressions, suspended and captured in a circle of communication between artist and viewer.

"I work mostly with the human figure because I find it the most ideal vehicle, for me, to explore human experiences. I produce images that I hope people will enjoy, and in them, find a meaning that is unique and personal."

Christopher's drawings, lithographs and paintings reflect years of disciplined training in the United States and Europe. He studied at the Academy of Art College in San Francisco and L'Academie de la Grande Chaumière in Paris. He earned a Bachelor of Fine Arts from the University of New Mexico. In addition, Christopher has worked at the Tamarind Institute, one of the few places in the world where the original techniques of lithography are practiced.

Christopher's formal concerns of strong design and clarity are melded with the textural feelings and activity of drawing and painting to produce compositions that do not pretend to reproduce the subject, but rather, distill the essence of it through meticulous craftsmanship.

The art of Christopher Bull has a timeless appeal and value, a quality recognized by the Museum of Albuquerque for his works were chosen in two consecutive years for Purchase Prizes. He creates pictures that are to be enjoyed as a quiet tribute to the beauty in life.

Artist Christopher Bull of Albuquerque, New Mexico, had his brochure professionally designed by Hal Johnson. "I recognized I wouldn't be able to do as good a job as a specialist." The tri-fold brochure, printed in black and white, features selected lithographs, photographs, drawings, and oil paintings, as well as a unique photograph of himself. He primarily uses the brochure as an informational gallery handout. For this reason he didn't have his address or phone printed on it. "Sometimes a gallery doesn't want this information on the piece because *it* wants to make the sale." If handing the brochure to a prospective buyer of his own, he includes a business card.

fessional affiliations, collections, and awards. Others communicate only the variety of work you do; purely promotional/informational brochures are devoted to your background and experience.

Consider these points when designing a brochure:

- It must fit in a client's 8½"x11" file drawer.
- Include at least one example of your work, preferably more.
- A photograph or self-portrait personalizes your message and gives the potential client a special visual reference.
- Do not include prices.
- If a self-mailer, one folded side must be blank so the brochure can be stapled or taped closed, addressed and stamped, and mailed without an envelope. The pa-

per must be heavy enough to sustain rough handling.
- Base your design and folding plan on standard paper sizes to save money at the printer.
- Other information in your brochure can include a brief description of each pictured work, original artwork sizes and media, and brief quotes from people or articles about you.

Letterhead and Envelopes

Letterhead is stationery imprinted with your name, address, and phone number, and possibly your logo and a brief descriptive phrase that defines you or your work. Letterhead might seem to you the least of your worries, but think again. In mailed submissions, your letterhead is the first "art" item the potential client sees. This same letterhead can serve for

"Les Trois Amis . . . The Three Friends" $85.00
A limited edition of 750. 16½"x25" on heavy weight art stock with 3"
border. Most prints have artist proofs available and certain numbers
on request.

"San Xavier del Bac."   "Camelback Mountain"

"Oak Creek Reflections"   "Grand Canyon"

© Roy Kerswill. Used
with permission.

HOW TO ADD A PERSONAL TOUCH

The six-page bro-
chure of Western art-
ist Roy Kerswill of
Jackson Hole, Wyo-
ming, is in the form of
a small booklet. The
cover is printed in
blue to match the
blue printing of his
stationery; it boasts a
self-portrait, which
personalizes the
marketing piece,
and Kerswill's distinc-
tive signature, which
he carries as a logo
through all of his ma-
terials. The booklet
features black-and-
white reproductions
of his detailed oil
paintings with ac-
companying text; a
color center section
portrays his print edi-
tions. He includes
prices on his prints in
the booklet because
he has established a
certain price range.
If the prints increase
in value, it's usually
in the secondary
market.

UPDATING A BROCHURE

This initial four-page
booklet brochure
created by Shirley
Gruen is filled with
full-color reproduc-
tions of her paintings
and drawings. The
inside cover presents
a self-portrait in
black and white and
brief biographical
material; detailed in-
formation accompa-
nies each painting.
Her second brochure
is a two-color tri-fold
with black-and-
white printing inside
and touches of blue
on the outside. Gruen
went to this brochure
because "it was less
costly and I knew it
would eventually
have to be updated.
I wanted something I
could hand to peo-
ple who came to my
studio and gallery
and I wanted an up-
date on my paintings
accepted into
shows." A third bro-
chure is a compro-
mise between the
two. "I put a little
more color in this one
and folded it horizon-
tally, so it is, in effect,
a resume."

© Shirley Gruen. Used with
permission.

Port Washington Flower 18x24

Shirley Scharen Gruen
STUDIO & GALLERY

103 East Grand Avenue
Port Washington, Wisconsin
284-2273

watercolors and acrylics
cards and notepaper
prints

Shirley Scharen Gruen

your resume, bills of sale, cover letters, and contracts.

Select quality paper. Not only does heavier paper feel richer, but you'll appreciate it if written information doesn't show through its matching envelope. Order matching blank sheets for correspondence extending beyond one page.

Select a readable typeface. If your name and address are difficult to decipher, busy clients won't take the time. Go through the printer's typeface sample book and decide which typeface visually communicates what you want to say about yourself. Generally speaking, serif typefaces are more traditional and readable, while sans serif typefaces are contemporary

SHOWING A VARIETY OF WORK

The tri-fold brochure of artist Anita Neal, Huntington Beach, California, contains eight examples of her work—an amazing amount considering the space available on an 8½" × 11" sheet of paper. But the design of the piece—the curved edges in the upper corners, the curved insets, and the content of the selected artworks— keep the page from appearing cluttered while conveying the range of Neal's style, subject matter, and media. Biographical material at the bottom presents insight to Neal's artistic background and she pro-

vides visual recognition through her logo. On the outside of the brochure are her photograph and artistic statement, her name in large, dramatic lettering, and the logo and graphic elements that match her stationery (see page 61). This brochure can be mailed or handed out.

© Anita Neal. Used with permission.

ANITA NEAL paintings may be figures, florals or landscapes...abstracts, moods, studies...or simply moments in time. They may be impressionistic, but mostly are realistic. All are self-assured and strong, created out of deep feeling and experience, born graphically with the sure hand of the designer, made impactful with exquisite color and technique.

The artist's works are shown in 60 galleries in the United States and Canada through Art Resources, Inc., and other paintings are in private collections here and in Europe.

In the spring of 1985 she was selected from thousands of candidates nationwide to be one of 60 artists in the New Art in New York exhibition at Parsons School of Design, Manhattan's most prestigious showcase for newcomers. At the same time, she exhibited by invitation in the California Artists Human Services show in the Wattles Mansion, Hollywood, California.

Neal paintings are in three additional juried shows: American Artists Magazine and Ariel Gallery, both in New York City; and the Texas Fine Arts Association's Gloria Laguna Museum, Austin. Her sculpture is in a juried show in New York City, the Pen and Brush Expo. Additional shows are Le Centre Internationale d'Art Contemporain, Paris, France; and Elan Galleries, Laguna Beach, California.

Ms. Neal, whose studios are in Huntington Beach and Fawnskin, California, currently has in work a limited edition bronze sculpture; diptychs; triptychs; a suite of five for a collector; the preparation of art for 3 shows and museums; and four additional commissions for individuals.

ANITA NEAL

and utilitarian. Script typefaces are fussy and nearly unreadable if filled with flourishes. Some typefaces lose their effectiveness when printed in a point size appropriate for stationery.

Remember these points when planning your letterhead:

■ Place your name and descriptive phrase, such as *watercolorist* or *portrait artist*, at the top of the letterhead to promote immediate identification.

■ Your address and phone number can be positioned at the top or the bottom. Include the area code in your phone number.

■ When selecting your descriptive phrase, use definitive descriptions, such as *wildlife watercolorist* or *pet portrait artist specializing in dogs*.

■ White, beige, or pale gray are the colors of choice for paper, but other pale shades are acceptable. Dark or garish colors connote insecurity and unprofessionalism in the business world and they make typed correspondence difficult to read.

■ If you're using colored ink for your letterhead, be aware of the final result of the ink's color combined with the paper's color. Every color combination has not only an aesthetic appeal, but also a "readability factor." The most readable color combination is black on yellow, followed by green, red, or black on white. Though these combinations might not appeal to you for your letterhead, keep the readability factor in mind as you make your ink and paper selection.

Your correspondence envelopes (#10 business size, 9½"x4⅛") should match your letterhead. Your name, address, and logo (if any) should be printed in the same typestyle and ink as the rest of your stationery. Large envelopes (9"x12") for mailed submissions can also be imprinted to match the letterhead if your finances allow.

Business Card
These 2"x3½" cards are invaluable for getting your name around. Even the most casual social setting creates the opportunity to present a new acquaintance with this brief communi-

HOW TO DESIGN MARKETING MATERIAL

When designing your printed marketing materials, keep these design basics in mind:

Contrast. Stress some elements more than others; this can be a contrast in size, shape, tone, texture, or direction.

Balance. Place elements with a sense of equilibrium; the weight of an element is the result of size, shape, and tone—large elements, irregular shapes, and dark elements appear heavier.

Proportion. Place elements in relationship to one another or to the design as a whole.

Rhythm. The eye will spot the orderly repetition of any element, whether line, shape, tone, or texture, and follow its pattern.

Unity. The total design should be coherent; individual elements should fit together.

Movement. Use the elements to direct the eye where you want it to go. You can influence eye movement by your element placement. Be aware of these patterns of eye movement:

■ A viewer sees the total product, not just elements.

■ After the eye's initial fixation on the design, it tends to move to the left and upward, exploring a page from this point in a clockwise direction.

■ The eye prefers horizontal movement.

■ A left position is preferred to a right; top is preferred to bottom.

cation about you and your work. They can also be attached to promotional materials lacking your address and phone number.

Because your business card so often represents you, design it with the same care and thought as you did your letterhead. Carry the same typeface and logo from your stationery. Utilize your business card to be more descriptive of the type of work you do. For example, if your letterhead contains only the description *Watercolorist*, you might continue the description on your business card by adding *specializing in wildlife*. However, if you aren't comfortable promoting yourself so narrowly, don't

Simplicity is the key word to Ed Hutchenreuther's stationery. Two sizes of lines give his materials a visual graphic element that carries through all of his pieces. A Sun City, Arizona, artist, Hutchenreuther works in pastels and pen and ink and has had his work in several galleries. When he first designed his stationery, he felt somewhat disappointed. "It didn't have anything that really knocked your eye out, or anything on it in the way of drawings and paintings. But the more I've seen it, the more I like it. I've had some nice compliments on it. Simplicity is sometimes the best thing."

© Ed Hutchenreuther. Used with permission.

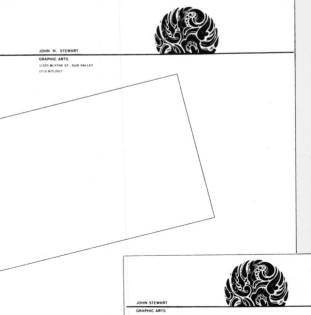

California artist John Stewart, a motion picture scenic artist for twelve years, has recently returned to showing his work in galleries. At one time his works hung in galleries nationwide, but time was at a premium with his movie work, and he produced fewer gallery pieces. His return to gallery work encompasses "talking with galleries on a one-to-one basis" and a hope that "I can take off for three or four months this year to get back to my fine-art work." The distinctive logo on Stewart's stationery and business card is an old design. "Probably '70-'71, and it was probably influenced a little bit by the late hippie movement. It was originally done for a school project . . . in commercial art. I've just continued to use it."

© 1982 Stewart Graphic Arts.

© Roy Kerswill. Used with permission.

Wyoming artist Roy Kerswill creates detailed oil paintings of the West, portraits, and print editions. So he has two types of letterhead to meet his marketing needs. Printed in blue on cream paper, his eye-catching logo unites all of the pieces. A small drawing on the envelope of a typical Western scene promotes his primary art interest. Kerswill keeps his clients current and his record-keeping straight through the use of this clever invoice. It makes it easy for the client to make a payment and know the exact balance. The logo and another Western scene tie the invoice in with his other marketing materials.

Anita Neal of Huntington Beach, California, a professional artist only since 1983, already has her paintings and sculpture in more than sixty galleries in the United States and Canada, in collections both here and in Europe, and accepted into numerous juried shows. In 1985, she was one of only sixty artists selected for the "New Art in New York" show at Parsons School of Design. Her stationery is printed in light burgundy ink on off-white paper and dramatically incorporates the intital "N" with a paint brush as a logo. The graphic lines create additional visual interest and keep the viewer's eyes anchored to her name.

© Anita Neal. Used with permission.

feel obligated to add this information.

If you're ordering only business cards, the same basic colors apply as for letterhead—white, beige, and pale gray. The typeface you select will be printed in a very small point size on these cards, so ask to see some samples from the printer to make sure the printing remains readable.

Resume

A resume is a historical document that summarizes your art-related background. Two types of resumes can be utilized: chronological and functional (see pages 66 and 67).

A *chronological resume* is a history of your accomplishments listed in chronological order, either from present-day backwards (called reverse chronological order) or from the earliest to the present day. The advantage to reverse chronological order is that it allows a client to immediately see your most recent accomplishments.

Group your information in categories, each with a self-explanatory heading. The categories should be pertinent to the market area you're approaching and should be a factual representation of your background. If you have more than twenty entries under one heading, divide it into subcategories. If you have fewer than three listings, integrate them into a broader category.

For example, a gallery director wants to know about other galleries that have carried your work. If your gallery list is longer than twenty entries, break them into subcategories, perhaps geographically (Midwest Galleries, Eastern Galleries), or by media (Galleries—Oils, Galleries—Watercolors). If your list doesn't warrant subcategories, list all under *Galleries* and, if appropriate, add a brief descriptive phrase.

All galleries that have exhibited your work for a given year can be listed together. If they are scattered nationwide, list the city and state location of each gallery. If all galleries are in the same city, put the city and state immediately below the main *Gallery* heading.

Begin with the category that is most important to the market you're approaching. Follow this first heading(s) with the categories that

Port Washington, New York, artist Mary Ann Heinzen, a full-time painter for three years, has her work in several galleries and has had great success in holding studio shows at her home. Her business cards are unique because each is an "original Heinzen." She orders plain cream-color cards in a matte finish with brown printing and then paints a quick watercolor "doodle" on each. Heinzen says "This may sound arduous, but I do batches of twenty-five to fifty whenever I find time. It also serves as a loosening-up exercise. This way, my cards always reflect my most current subject matter and style. I find people are delighted to receive them, feeling that they have been given an actual piece of my work—sort of a free sample."

© Mary Ann Heinzen. Used with permission.

RAY FRIESZ (714) 643-3063
28182 RUBICON CT., LAGUNA NIGUEL, CA 92656

The simple black-on-white signature of California artist Ray Friesz captures the energy and texture of his paintings so well that it makes its own statement on his business cards. Described as belonging to the "abstract-impressionism-expressionistic-realism" school of art, Friesz pours, throws, and splatters acrylic paint into landscapes and seascapes, then develops each painting further by defining forms and highlighting the foreground. He sells through galleries and home studio shows; his works are also in corporate and private collections. He enjoys the contacts developed in home studio sales. "Every artist has the opportunity to develop an 'inner sanctum'—fans who collect his or her work and like private or group invitations to the artist's home studio. From these I make sales and receive commissions."

Though Thom Whitbeck of Houston, Texas, doesn't paint full-time, he's sold out of current paintings and has a waiting list for commissions. He's tried several different kinds of business cards. The first was a very simple one on white paper; the second included a pen and ink drawing that met with some response. But this full-color business card picturing one of his paintings has met with the most enthusiastic response of all. "I've had it for two-and-a-half years and had quite a few reprints made. A lot of times people will ask if they can have another card, just to show and give to somebody else." A watercolorist, Whitbeck chose this painting for his card because it's "a good representative example of the medium that I use, the type of work I do, and

the style and feeling I try to put in my painting. I end up talking more about my work by showing people what I do than if I just made the simple statement 'I'm an artist.' "

294-8177
Beverly June Stewart
Oriental Brush Painting
1133 Marigold Dr. N.E.
Albuquerque, N.M. 87122

The business card of New Mexico artist Beverly Stewart immediately conveys her specialization in and love of Oriental brush painting. Printed black on white, the card complements her informational flyer (see page 41) and is placed on the backs of her paintings. Stewart was introduced to Sumi-e, the art of Oriental brush painting, when she lived in Japan for three years in the 1950s. She's continued to study and develop her art in Europe and the United States and was selected to study at the Zhejiang Academy of Fine Arts in Hangzhou, China, in 1984. Exhibitions of her work have been held here and in Europe, including the Sumi-e Society of America, Inc. in New York; she's competed in both local and national competitions, winning national awards, and has her work in local galleries.

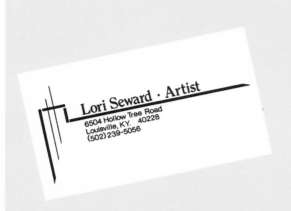

© Lori Seward. Used with permission.

Lori Seward of Louisville, Kentucky, had been trying for about a year to design her business materials. "Finally I just sat down one day and designed it in about ten minutes. I wanted something simple and crisp looking." Seward's black-on-white design grabs the viewer's attention and holds it on her name—an ideal way to increase name recognition. Seward currently receives oil portrait commissions primarily through word of mouth. But she created her distinctive design for her letterhead and business card because she eventually wants to contact galleries and printers. "I believe it's more professional to have a business card and letterhead that match to get their attention."

Printed in deep burgundy ink on cream stock, the business card of Rosalind Lipscomb is filled with her sweeping signature. A portrait artist from Americus, Georgia, Lipscomb chose red for the printing because "I usually like to see some form of red in my portraits. For example, in a man's portrait, I wouldn't have the red on his lips, but might place a small amount in his necktie. My signature isn't red on my paintings; I use a color that's appropriate. But I tried to tie the signature and the use of the color red into the business card."

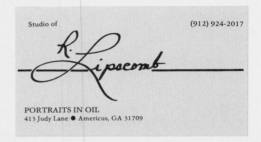

© Rosalind Lipscomb. Used with permission.

S.P. w/Ruby-Throated Hummingbird. Photograph for business card design © 1982 by Den Navrat. Private collection of the artist.

The captivating image on Den Navrat's business card is a photograph he took himself. Navrat explains, "I was building a house with a skylight in the garage. In the fall, a ruby-throated hummingbird got trapped in the skylight. I crawled up a 24' ladder, got the hummingbird to alight on my hand several times, and took a sequence of pictures." A full-time professor of art at Dickinson State College, North Dakota, Navrat is currently specializing in mixed media handmade paper for his own works. He's selling through a Chicago gallery, exhibiting throughout the Midwest, and entering competitions. To date he's had more than 280 exhibitions. He is also art director for Mind's Eye Gallery, the campus art gallery, and finds that with three careers, he's developed a realistic attitude about his artwork: "I'm doing what I can and trying to get better at it while building up an inventory of work and slides."

convey your art-related background and professionalism. Other categories may include awards, collections, shows/exhibitions, commissions, education, and publications. Treat each of these categories as outlined for *Galleries*. Personal history, such as outside interests, marital status, and health status, goes last, but is completely optional. Most clients couldn't care less if you're married and enjoy soccer.

A chronological resume must be concise. One-sentence descriptions at most should accompany each listing. With the space limitations of a resume, lengthy explanations mean other pertinent information is being dropped.

A *functional resume* uses brief summarizing paragraphs about your art career or art-related experiences rather than items listed in a specific order. This resume is ideal for new artists or artists marketing their work for the first time.

For this resume, headings are normally broad by necessity. For example, if you've exhibited work in only one booth show and one co-op gallery, the heading for this paragraph might be *Previous Sales*. This broad category now allows you to draw in *all* experience related to the topic of the heading—the type of buyer that liked your work; how these experiences helped you to grow as an artist; or what the experience led to (a new technique, subject matter, medium), thanks to viewers' comments. Your experience might be from many places—life, volunteer work, or schooling—but use it to make you and your art interesting and exciting to a potential client. You can also include travel and hobby experiences if they legitimately relate to and promote your art experience.

If you don't have any formal art education, write a paragraph about workshops and seminars you've attended and any well-known person you studied under. Head this category *Art-Related Education*.

Keep your paragraphs short and language descriptive. Include a statement about art goals or an art analysis/description if you desire, but don't crowd out other important information.

A resume should be one page, definitely no more than two. Always begin with your name, address, and phone number with area code. Make your resume visually attractive and interesting through underlining, boldface type, capital letters, indenting, and bullets. Be consistent; if you use boldface type for one category heading, use it for all similar headings.

A resume is not a static document. You can set up categories in any professional-sounding manner you wish that shows you to your best advantage. Utilize your market research to tie your information to your specific market area.

If you have letterhead, use it for your resume. Otherwise use white, beige or light gray paper. Your resume should match your business card and stationery as much as possible to create a unified package.

Your resume does not have to be professionally typeset and printed, especially if you anticipate changing it frequently. A printed resume gives the most professional appearance but is the most expensive. You can type it on white paper and photocopy it onto your letterhead or matching blank stationery. Check the possibility of a word-processing service, especially if you anticipate frequent use and changes. Use your resume in leave-behind packets, for in-person interviews, and in mailing packages.

Flyer

If you think of a brochure as a sixty-second commercial, then a flyer is a thirty-second one. A flyer is a single sheet of paper or lightweight cardboard with your most vital information printed on one side (see page 68). It must be eye-catching, dynamic, and designed for immediate visual impact. Carry your logo or distinctive graphic element onto your flyer.

To convey your art style, a flyer must contain at least one example of your work. Brief written text can also be included, but it's perfectly acceptable if it contains only your name, address, and phone number, with the artwork speaking for itself. A flyer is not meant to communicate everything about you and your work; rather, it keeps your name and work in front of a potential client's eyes and in mind. A self-portrait or photograph can also be included.

This multi-purpose promotional tool is frequently mailed as a follow-up to previous contacts to inform them about your most recent work or perhaps a change you've made. It can also be used in a mailing package, be handed out at shows/exhibitions, accompany work in sales outlets, act as an announcement, and be placed in a leave-behind package.

If your flyer is to be self-mailed, choose heavy, good quality paper since it must endure mailing conditions. The flyer can be very effectively and inexpensively executed in black and white.

Mailer

The mailer performs many of the same functions as a flyer but is approximately postcard size or slightly larger and is printed on lightweight cardboard stock to withstand mailing. An example of your work appears on one side,

TWO TYPES OF RESUMES

These two samples convey the difference and similarity between the two types of resumes, chronological and functional. The chronological resume (left), like the functional resume, categorizes resume topics, but simply lists specific events by date. The functional resume pulls in life experience to complement art-related events and details them in short paragraphs.

```
                          YOUR NAME
                         Your Address
                         City State Zip
                      Phone with Area Code



GALLERIES

    1988

        Coleridge Art Gallery, Boulder, Colorado    Watercolors

        Landview Ridge Gallery, Mountainview, Montana    Watercolors

        Simon Gallery of Fine Art, Simpson, California    Acrylics

    1987

        Creekwater Gallery, Stoney, Maine    Oils

        Fine Arts of Illinois, Chicago, Illinois    Watercolors


AWARDS

    1988

        Best of Show, Topeka Watercolor Invitational Show, Topeka, Kansas

        Second Prize, Cincinnati Fine Arts Exhibit, Cincinnati, Ohio

        First Prize, Crestview Regional Art Exhibit, Crestview, Louisiana

    1987

        First Prize, New Mexico Fine Art Invitational, Las Cruces, New Mexico

        Best of Show, Sixth Regional Exhibition, Louisville, Kentucky

        Honorable Mention, Washington State Exhibition, Ridge, Washington


COLLECTIONS

    Mayor and Mrs. Fred Smith, Landview, Wisconsin

    Mr. and Mrs. Price Simpson, Washington, DC

    Mr. and Mrs. Laughton Jameson, Albuquerque, New Mexico

    Sandra Connell, Chicago, Illinois



-- Other suggested headings are: MAJOR JURIED SHOWS, CORPORATE COLLECTIONS,
COMMISSIONS, MAJOR INVITATIONAL SHOWS, TRAVEL, LECTURES/TEACHING, PROFESSIONAL
AFFILIATIONS, REVIEWS, PUBLICATIONS, SPECIAL PROJECTS, EDUCATION, PERSONAL
INFORMATION, PHILOSOPHY.
```

with or without your name, address, and phone number; the reverse side is utilized for the addressee's name and address. If your name and address don't appear with your artwork, make certain they appear on this side.

Mailers can be printed in black and white or color. If a logo or consistent design appears on your materials, include it on your mailers to maintain continuity of your artistic identity.

This promotional tool allows you to relay a personal message, such as confirmation of an appointment, announcement of a recent award or your next show, an example of your most recent work and where it can be seen, or even a holiday greeting. Excellent as follow-up reminders, mailers can also be included in mailing and leave-behind packages and used as handouts.

```
                        YOUR NAME
                       Your Address
                      City State Zip
                   Phone with Area Code



    STATEMENT

        Also called a Philosophy; a paragraph that states the strongest and
        most unique qualities of your art; also a description.

    EXHIBITIONS

        Rather than breaking these down into specific areas, such as Galleries,
        Awards, Major Juried Shows, and so on, list all times your work has been
        exhibited anywhere for any reason.  Discuss all positive aspects of the
        experiences -- comments from the public and from important people, number
        of sales, your growth as an artist.

    EDUCATION

        If you have a college degree, say so; if not, don't worry about it.
        Write about any educational experience that's art-related, such as
        workshops, seminars you've attended, art classes taken; name prominent
        instructors you've studied under; any school project you contributed to
        in an artistic way.  This category can also be called ART-RELATED
        EDUCATION or EDUCATION-RELATED EXPERIENCE.

    TRAVEL

        If you've traveled and it led to an art-related experience, such as
        visiting art museums in Europe or in the U.S., write briefly how this
        experience affected your work, your insight as an artist, your growth
        as an artist.

    LECTURES/TEACHING

        Any time you've given a demonstration or taught a class, this is
        valuable art-related experience.  Write about how your skill/expertise
        in your medium or technique qualified you to demonstrate or teach and
        bring in any unusual talent you shared with others.

    SPECIAL PROJECTS

        Include here any project you've been involved in that required your art
        talent, such as a volunteer community project or a contribution to a
        nonprofit or civic organization.

    COMMISSIONS

        If anyone has ever asked you to paint something specifically for him/her,
        it's a commission.  Include it if you can relate it to a positive aspect
        of your art career or growth as an artist.

    PERSONAL STATEMENT

        (Optional)  This is a statement about yourself -- your goals, aspirations,
        how far you've come, what you've learned about yourself, how you believe
        you've evolved and developed as an artist.
```

HOW TO GRAB ATTENTION

Beverly Stewart's striking flyer is printed in full color on a black background and shows off her Oriental brush painting style and subject matter. Stewart had it printed specifically to drop off at galleries. It gives them a little information on her; a photograph further personalizes the flyer. She admits that she's "a prolific painter." After moving to Albuquerque, New Mexico, she has "done very well locally keeping galleries supplied. There's no work sitting on the floor at home that isn't being shown."

Beverly June Stewart

Beverly Stewart was introduced to Sumié, the art of oriental brush painting, in 1956 when she lived in Tokyo, Japan. She became enchanted with the beautiful simplicity of the paintings which approaches the abstract concept of art. During this period she also received her teacher's certificate in the Sogetsu School of Japanese flower arranging, which enabled her to develop her own concept of oriental design.

She studied oil and acrylics when she lived in Norway, and continued in this medium with Marian Carey in Newport, Rhode Island. She returned to the oriental medium when she lived in Wash.,DC, where her teachers included Roddy McLean, Lui Sang Wong, and the internationally known Henry Wo Yue-kee, who Bev considers her master. Henry is well known as the "lotus artist", from the Ling Nam School of southern China. Her international experience came to a climax in 1984 when she was chosen to study at the Zhejiang Academy of Fine Arts in Hangzhou, China.

Bev now lives in Albuquerque, New Mexico where she continues to paint and enjoys teaching and showing her work.

Her work has been exhibited and won awards in the United States and Europe, and is included in the Albuquerque High Collection at the Albuquerque Museum.

Her exhibitions include:
Sumié Society of America, Inc., New York City, New York
L'Erbisoeul Galeria, Mons, Belgium
Supreme Headquarters Allied Powers Europe
National League of Penwomen
The New Mexico State Fair
Artist's Alpine Holiday, Ouray, Colorado
Brush and Palette Club, Western Colorado Center for the Arts
Black Canyon 25th Exhibition, Colorado
15th National Art Show, La Junta, Colorado

Studio Address:
1133 Marigold Dr. NE
Albuquerque, New Mexico 87122
(505) 294-8177

stewart

Reply Card

You enclose a reply card with mailed submissions to encourage a prompt reply from a potential client. Frequently the reply card is an ordinary self-addressed stamped postcard you create yourself, but you can also design a card to coordinate with the rest of your materials.

If you're using a postcard, responses appropriate to your client or market area should be typed on the back so that the client has only to check off a response, fill in the blanks, and drop the card in the mail. A reply card works especially well when no other materials are to be returned. It increases your chance of receiving an indication of follow-up action you can take.

When composing your responses, put yourself in the client's place and focus the reply card as much as possible on responses appropriate to this field.

Some sample responses are:

( ) We'd like to see more of your work; contact us for an appointment.
( ) We will keep your samples on file for possible future consideration.
( ) We can't handle any new artists right now; contact us again in _____ months.
( ) Your work isn't appropriate for our outlet; your samples are being returned.
( ) We aren't interested, but thank you for thinking of us.

Be sure to type blanks at the bottom for the client's name, company name, and the date so you know who it's from and when it was acted upon.

SASE

Enclose a self-addressed, stamped envelope (SASE) in mailed submissions when you want your samples returned. It isn't a guarantee of their return, but without it, it's guaranteed they won't be returned. No client has the time or money to address and stamp envelopes to soliciting artists.

One important point to remember regarding the return of samples: *No one is obliged by law to return any unsolicited materials.* Most clients make a concerted effort to return materials an artist has requested, but not all. Send out samples with the idea that you hope to get them back but you'll survive if you don't. If you feel losing those samples is a real setback, rethink what you're sending. Perhaps you need to acquire more duplicates or go to a less expensive sample type. Be sure the return envelope is large enough to handle the samples you've sent and carries sufficient postage.

Information Sheet

An information sheet is an 8½″ x 11″ sheet of paper containing supplementary information on the samples you've submitted. Numbers on your individual samples should match the numbers on your information sheet. Listed here are pertinent facts regarding the artwork, your thinking in creating the artwork, any awards or prizes it's won, prestigious exhibitions, and so on. An information sheet is especially useful with mailed submissions when you're not present to fill in details

Type the information sheet and photocopy it on your letterhead or blank stationery sheets. Be sure it contains correct grammar and is easy to follow.

Leave-Behind

This is one of those items that is exactly what it sounds like—a single piece or a packet of material that you leave behind with a client after an in-person interview. Information on the style, medium, and subject matter of your art, as well as your background and experience as a fine artist, can then be kept on file. The material serves as a reminder that you'd like to have your work handled or purchased by the client.

A leave-behind can be *several* of your promotional/marketing pieces working together as a cohesive unit. It can be a combination of a brochure or a flyer, resume, business card, and one or more actual samples of your work. Include a visual example of your work and written information. It's best to let the client keep a slide or photograph on file, but, if the potential of this client is slim and your finances are tight, a printed example of your work, such as appears on a brochure, flyer, or mailer, suffices.

Paintings by
Margaret E. Rosenberg
Cornerstone Gallery of Fine Arts
Railroad Street, Falls Village, Connecticut

May 16 -31, 1987

2:00 - 4:00 p.m. daily except Mondays

Informal Opening

Saturday, May 16, 1987

4:00 - 7:00 p.m.

For information call (203) 824-0390

Paintings by
Margaret E. Rosenberg
Cornerstone Gallery of Fine Arts
Railroad Street, Falls Village, Connecticut

Thursday through Sunday

April 16 - 31, 1988

2:00 - 4:00 p.m. daily except Mondays

Informal Opening

Saturday, April 16, 1988

5:00 - 7:00 p.m.

For information call (203) 824-0390

Peggy Rosenberg
47 Pamela Drive
Milford, Connecticut 06460
(203) 783-1934 (203) 874-2136

© 1987
Margaret E.
Rosenberg.
Used with
permission.

© 1988
Margaret E.
Rosenberg.
Used with
permission.

Connecticut artist Peggy Rosenberg used these mailers to announce openings at the gallery that handles her works and at a local library. Printed in black and white on cardboard stock that's glossy on one side, they were quickly produced at a printing shop. "On one of the mailers I had access to a camera and was able to give the printer my own halftone of the painting's photograph. On others, I just walked in with a black-and-white photograph."

Artist Linda Kirsten Cole has been painting about twenty-one years and has her own studio and gallery. She uses this 3½" × 5½" black-and-white card for two purposes: "It's my business card. It won't get lost as much as the smaller ones that people tuck away. I turn it over, rule it in half and use it as a postcard when I want to send out a reminder to pick up work or announce a show." Cole, who lives in Maryland, New York, not only sells from her own gallery, but through two galleries in Florida, booth shows, and commissions. She's also had some of her paintings reproduced as prints and says "They're selling very, very well. Locally, the last art show I did, about half of my sales were my prints. I think the prints were one of the best things I've done because they help get my work out to another market."

THE COLE STUDIO

Watercolors by
LINDA KIRSTEN COLE

Goodyear Lake
607-432-3546

Lake Shore Drive South
R.D. 1, Box 1306A
Maryland, New York 12116

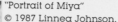

"Portrait of Miya"
© 1987 Linnea Johnson.

"Honey Hearts, Honey?"
© 1987 Linnea Johnson.

Linnea Johnson of Port Angeles, Washington, avidly promotes her work. One of the tools she uses are full-color postcards of her works. "I send them out with handprinted invitations for opening receptions. In fact, one of them intrigued the *Port Townsend Leader*'s art critic enough that she called for an interview and wrote a nice article about me and my work. I plan on using them as invitations for other shows I have scheduled, and always have the postcards and copies of the article with me to give to anyone who shows the least bit of interest in my work. When I use one of them as a business card, I add my phone number and the location of my next showing." The back of the postcards shows Johnson's address; the size, title and medium of the artwork; and her copyright notice.

Susan Greaves had these postcards printed to match her stationery (see page 20) to add to her marketing materials. They can fill a variety of purposes—announcements, invitations, reminders, or simply a personal greeting. Each time one is sent out, it brings the client's attention to her logo and name. Greaves developed her *Painting Notes* from an idea she'd read in an article. "With my stationery design as a starting point, some computer printing, cut-and-paste technique, and a photocopier, I've made forms to attach to each of my works. I include a description of the painting, any anecdote that might be interesting, comments by other artists or jurors, and awards won. This seems to stimulate collectors, provide galleries with more background material, and make even older pieces more attractive to buyers."

© Susan F. Greaves. Used with permission.

Keep these pieces together in a standard pocket folder or custom-design your own folder to coordinate with the rest of your materials. Clear plastic pockets also work well, as do clear acetate sheets held together with a plastic spine; all can be purchased at stationery and art supply stores. Be sure all materials fit the standard 8½" x 11" file drawer.

Labels

Self-adhesive labels, imprinted with your name, address, and logo, serve a multitude of purposes and also give your name frequent visibility. Small labels with only your name and address can be used to label the backs of samples as well as finished artwork. For mailed submissions or shipment of work, use large labels that contain your name, address, and logo *and* provide room for addressing.

Both of these accessories increase logo recognition and name identification and coordinate your entire marketing package even further.

Writing Copy that Sells

Brochures have room for the most written text; here you can expand on your best qualities. Don't overdo, but don't miss out on these occasions to promote yourself. When creating written text, remember to:

■ Brush up on grammar and punctuation. Your professional image is dealt a severe blow if misspellings and haphazard punctuation appear in your text.

■ Use descriptive language. Avoid provoking nausea, but look for sentences where more active or descriptive words could bring them alive. Selectively use a thesaurus to find synonyms for lazy verbs, nouns, adjectives, and adverbs. For example, do you consider your work "dramatic"? Then it can also be vivid, expressive, powerful, striking, moving, or touching. Do you "see"? Then you can also envision, visualize, imagine, conceive, image, or picture.

■ Form sentences that emphasize the words you want noticed.

■ Be brief. This text is a selling tool, not a life history. Favor short sentences.

■ Organize your information before you begin. Return to the lists containing the good points of your work and your qualities. Use these as a basis for your text.

■ Group similar facts and ideas together.

■ Plan your writing so readers pick up the message immediately and understand it completely.

■ Be sure *everything* you write is proofread before it's printed; find a knowledgeable friend or ask if your printer offers this service.

If you don't feel entirely confident with your copywriting skills, contact a professional writer for help. Perhaps networking has put you in touch with a writer who will draft your material or edit what you've written, either for a reduced fee or in exchange for one of your paintings.

HOW TO EXPLAIN
WHAT YOU SHOW

RAY SMITH
3399 Main Street
Hancock, Maine 30339
205/555-2669

INFORMATION SHEET

(1) "Blue Vision" Oil 12" X 48" Completed in 1987
Executed in a semi-abstract technique, "Blue Vision" is the ocean
off the coast of Hancock, Maine, a small fishing village. The power
and majesty of the ocean is tempered by the serenity of the prevalence
of blue and green. The white highlights strategically and consciously
splattered throughout the canvas suggest the spray of the ocean breaking
along the rugged coastline. AWARDS: Best of Show, Maine National Art
Exhibition, 1987; First Place, Abstract Art Show, New York, 1988.
Canvas on wood stretcher bars; framed in silver aluminum.

(2) "Mist of the Seashore" Oil 24" X 48" Completed in 1987
A painting that captures the lure of the sea in fog, "Mist of the
Seashore" wraps the viewer in shades of gray and white with a hint
of the blue-green of the ocean sweeping from the bottom. Executed
in an impressionistic-abstract style, the painting glistens and becomes the focal point of every showing. EXHIBITIONS: One-person
show, Sunset Gallery, Back Bay, Vermont; Group Show, Country Gallery,
Bangor, Maine; Group Show, Sampson Gallery, New York City. AWARDS:
First Place, Ohio Regional Abstract Exhibition, 1988.

(3) "Purple Nightshade" Oil 24" X 36" Completed in 1988
A dark, moody painting that comes alive when the viewer relates to
the ship that's suggested caught in the huge swell of a stormy ocean.

This labeled slide (below) is coordinated to an information sheet by using a reference number in the lower right-hand corner of the front of the slide. Always type your information sheet, preferably on your letterhead, and include as much information about each artwork that's important for the reviewer to know—awards it's received, reviews that specifically mention the work, a special technique you used, and so on. If desired, prices can be placed on the information sheet, especially if you compile a new sheet with each showing so that outdated prices don't appear. If they aren't placed here, a separate price list can be typed.

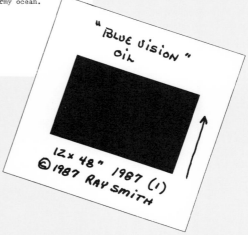

CHAPTER FOUR CHECKLISTS

Effective marketing tools available to you are:
- [ ] Art samples
- [ ] Brochure
- [ ] Letterhead and envelope
- [ ] Business card
- [ ] Resume
- [ ] Flyer
- [ ] Mailer
- [ ] Reply card
- [ ] Labels
- [ ] Information sheet

So that slides and photographs accurately represent your work, make sure that:
- [ ] Color is true and the contrast is good for black-and-white work
- [ ] The image fills the frame and is centered
- [ ] Background is clean and neutral
- [ ] Edges are straight
- [ ] Focus is sharp
- [ ] There is no glare or "hot spots"

Correct labeling of samples includes:
- [ ] Title of artwork
- [ ] Medium
- [ ] Size of artwork
- [ ] Year date of completion
- [ ] Copyright notice
- [ ] Arrow indicating orientation
- [ ] Reference number (optional)
- [ ] Name
- [ ] Address
- [ ] Telephone number with area code

When hiring a photographer, check that the photographer:
- [ ] Has previous (preferably extensive) experience in shooting two-dimensional art
- [ ] Will discuss fees before shooting work
- [ ] Will establish terms for re-shooting unacceptable slides or photographs

- [ ] Allows you to own negatives
- [ ] Presents samples of work for inspection
- [ ] Preferably is recommended by other artists

To photograph your own works, you'll need:
- [ ] 35mm SLR camera with 50mm or macro lens
- [ ] Tripod
- [ ] Film—Kodak Ektachrome 50 Prof (50 ASA) for color slides; Kodacolor VR-G 100 (100 ASA) for color prints; Plus-X Pan (125 ASA) for black-and-white prints
- [ ] Two floodlights
- [ ] Floodlight reflectors and stands
- [ ] Kodak Gray Card and color scale
- [ ] Cable release
- [ ] Neutral background material
- [ ] Correcting filter (optional)

A brochure should meet the following requirements:
- [ ] Is a pamphlet, booklet or multifold printed piece
- [ ] Contains large amount of space for artwork and text
- [ ] Contains at least one art example
- [ ] Stands by itself or works with other pieces
- [ ] Is your highest financial investment of all printed material
- [ ] Fits into an 8½"x11" file drawer
- [ ] Designed on standard paper sizes to save money
- [ ] Designed with folding in mind
- [ ] Includes your name and possibly your address and phone number with area code
- [ ] Carries logo or design from letterhead to unify materials

Your letterhead and envelope design should:
- [ ] Communicate your name, address, phone number and brief description
- [ ] Advertise who you are and what you do

☐ Be printed on the best paper you can afford

☐ Be printed preferably on white, beige or pale gray paper

☐ Feature readable typeface

☐ Show your address and phone at top or bottom of page

☐ Feature same logo and typeface as other printed materials

The ideal business card:

☐ Is standard 2" × 3½" size for easy filing

☐ Is imprinted with same logo and typeface as letterhead

☐ Has a typeface that is readable

☐ Is a color that matches letterhead

☐ Includes expanded descriptive phrasing, if desired

☐ Is usable for both business and social contacts

☐ Is attachable to other marketing materials to provide address and/or phone number

Your resume:

☐ Can be chronological or functional

☐ Is a history of your art-related background

☐ Should be confined to one page, two at most

☐ Provides information specific to your target market areas

☐ Should be typed or printed on letterhead or same paper stock

☐ Should begin with name, address, and phone number

☐ Exhibits consistency through underlinings, boldface type, capital letters and indenting

☐ Is concise

☐ Uses descriptive language

☐ Is an honest representation of your career

☐ Receives regular updates

☐ Lists your name, address (with zip code) and phone number (with area code)

Your flyer:

☐ Is a single sheet of paper

☐ Contains only vital information

☐ Possesses at least one art example

☐ Can also contain self-portrait or photograph

☐ Is designed to be eye-catching

☐ Includes brief self-promotional message

☐ Is usable in mailing packages, leave-behinds or for follow-up mailings

☐ Contains logo or graphic design element to unify materials

☐ Can be printed in black and white or color

☐ Can be self-mailed

☐ Can accompany artwork in sales outlets

The mailer:

☐ Is approximately postcard size or slightly larger

☐ Is printed on lightweight cardboard for self-mailing

☐ Contains an example of your artwork on one side

☐ Reverse side is for addressee

☐ Can be printed in black and white or color

☐ Contains logo or graphic design element to unify materials

☐ Is used for appointment confirmations, announcements, change of address or phone, greetings

☐ Can be placed in mailed packages, leave-behinds and used as handouts and for reminder mailings

☐ Lists your name, address (with zip code) and phone number (with area code)

The leave-behind:

☐ Is a packet of materials left with client after an in-person review

☐ Lists your name, address (with zip code) and phone number (with area code)

☐ Is filed by client as a reminder

☐ Contains several marketing tools working as a unit

☐ Should contain at least one slide or photograph

☐ Is held together with a folder or acetate sheet

☐ Should fit 8½" × 11" file drawer

THE MARKETING PLAN

This chapter is about action. You have found your market and chosen your tools. It's time for step five—initiating the marketing plan.

For artists who have never marketed their paintings before, much of the initial action deals with the mechanics of actually producing your marketing tools, such as selecting artwork to be reproduced as samples, contacting a photographer to shoot your work, obtaining price quotes from printers, writing copy for a brochure, and so on. If you already possess some marketing materials, however, set aside time to evaluate them for their effectiveness and how well they reflect who you are as an artist today. If they're still satisfactory, review the marketing tools in the previous chapter and determine how you can build on the older pieces to round out your package. Match your new materials' paper color, quality and typestyle to the older materials. If your pieces are unsatisfactory, simply throw them out, don't look back, and start over.

You can keep track of both these production activities and the information gathered after you begin contacting clients. All it takes is a little organization.

TOOLS TO ORGANIZE MARKETING

Since marketing involves both short- and long-term goals, you'll need to keep track of what needs to be done day by day. Here are some tools that will help you organize your marketing efforts.

The Marketing Calendar

The marketing calendar is an organizational tool that eliminates procrastination and a haphazard, ineffective marketing program. To begin your marketing calendar, buy or draw a large calendar for the year, a sheet for each month. Simple empty squares with the date in the corner suffice.

As items need to be designed, picked up at the printer, and so on, mark each task on the

HOW TO KEEP TRACK

Marketing calendars can be as simple as this one—the primary consideration is to have sufficient room each day to write in daily marketing and self-promotional tasks. Though not every date is filled in here, promise yourself now to devote a part of each day to a business aspect no matter how minor. The business side of art soon becomes a routine habit and the calendar keeps you organized and directed.

MONTH JUNE YEAR

				1 CALL PHOTOGRAPHER - SLIDES - NEW WORK	2 CALL PRINTERS - QUOTES - BROCHURE	3	4
5	6	7 TO PHOTOGRAPHER - 2:30	8	9	10 P/U 9X12 ENVELOPES	11 ART ASSOCIATION MEETING - 1:00	
12	13	14 COMPILE GALLERY PACKAGES - PACKAGE #1 (SEE MASTER CARD)	15	16 MAIL GALLERY PACKAGES	17	18	
19	20 CALL SUNSET GALLERY - SEE INDEX CARD	21	22	23	24 P/U SLIDE SHEETS	25	
26	27	28 APPT: 10:00 SUNSET GALLERY	29	30			

HOW TO GET ORGANIZED

Maintain a file of marketing cards on each client and you'll always know exactly where you stand. A simple glance at the card let's you know what action has been taken and where you want to go from here. The amount of detail you place on each card is a personal decision, but working in conjunction with your marketing calendar keeps your marketing plan on the right track.

CHARISMA ART IN THE PARK
CONTACT: FRANK SMITH, CHAIRMAN
29389 WINDING WAY
BRENDON IL 23412
(608) 555-8228

5.2.88 - SLIDES SENT FOR JURYING
6.7.88 - ACCEPTANCE RECEIVED
7.15/18 - SHOW DATES

TRI-STATE WATERCOLOR SHOW
CONTACT: HELEN BURNS
c/o HOLDEN WATERCOLOR SOCIETY
21 PRIVATE DRIVE
SAMPSON IL 32118
9.2 - PROSPECTUS RECEIVED
11.3 - SLIDES SENT (DEADLINE 11/15) - JURYING
12.15 - REJECTED - SLIDES RETURNED
(NO REASON GIVEN)

SUNRISE GALLERY   DIRECTOR:
49230 PACKING ROAD   SUSAN JAMES
MITCHUM WI 29333
(606) 555-2000

1/31 - INPERSON VISIT (SEE EVALUATION CARD)
2/6 - PHONED FOR APPOINTMENT - SPOKE W/
SUSAN
2/15 - APPOINTMENT - REVIEW 2:30 PM

calendar so that no marketing aspect is overlooked. When you begin to contact clients, use the marketing calendar to assign a day to phone for appointments, to record appointment times, and, following the interviews, to schedule a day about six weeks away on which to do a reminder or follow-up mailing. By assigning a date for these mailings *immediately*, you won't let six months slip away before remembering to follow through.

If you're marketing through the mail, gather your package materials and use the marketing calendar to assign a day to collate and mail them and to follow up with phone calls or reminder mailings. If a client returns a reply card and suggests contact in six months, mark your calendar at once with, "New mailing package to Mr. Jones, Nouveau Art Gallery. See index card."

The marketing calendar is vital to organizing booth shows and juried competitions. Record deadlines for slides, when to ship accepted works, show dates, designated date for notification of winners, dates for picking up returned works, even when you wrote for and received prospectuses. If entering numerous shows/competitions, color-code the information pertaining to the same show/competition.

Marketing and Master Cards

Marketing cards and master cards are more tools that organize and provide quick, easy access to pertinent information.

HOW TO USE A MASTER CARD

MASTER CARD

PACKAGE No. 1 :   COVER LETTER FOR GALLERY DIRECTORS
RESUME FOR GALLERIES
BUSINESS CARD
SAMPLES: THREE SLIDES OF WATERCOLOR
LANDSCAPES
"AUTUMN FARMHOUSE"
"PASTURE WIND"
"DAISIES IN SUMMER SUN"

BRICK OVEN GALLERY   DIRECTOR:
9 MAIN ST.   RUSSELL KING
SUNSET   VT 46120
(821) 314·1122

INITIAL CONTACT: PHONE 4·21·88
BROCHURE RECEIVED: 5·3·88
MAILING SENT: PACKAGE No.1 - 5·8·88

This is an example of how a master card works together with the marketing card. The information on the master card allows you to simply note which package was sent to a client; you don't end up sending a client the same slides or marketing materials again. The client's always receiving fresh images of your work and has the opportunity to see a greater range and depth of your talent.

Marketing cards are 3″x5″ index cards that list the substance of and results of each contact. When setting appointments for in-person reviews, record on the marketing card the name of the contact person, business name, address, phone number, date of call, and the result of the call. Are you supposed to call back? Mark your calendar, "Call Mr. Smith, XYZ Gallery, re: setting appt. See index card."

When an interview is completed, record the date, results, and your impressions. One or two words do it, just enough to refresh your memory. If you left behind slides in a packet for a client's files, note the titles of the slides' paintings. This allows you to submit fresh images through reminder mailings.

Marketing cards should also be kept on mailed submissions. As with in-person reviews, record on your card or computer the name of the contact person, business name, address, phone, and date of mailing.

A master card (usually a 5″x8″ index card) describes the samples and printed pieces included in the mailing. The master card might read: "Package 1: samples—three slides of oil florals: 'Morning Mist,' 'Peonies,' 'Garden Sunshine'; resume geared to gallery directors; cover letter for gallery directors; business card." The marketing card of clients who received this mailing would simply state "Package 1"; and you have on record exactly what was received.

If you use reply cards and receive a response, staple the reply card directly to the marketing card; note on the marketing card any further action to be taken. If any response is received from a mailed submission, note the response and the date on the client's marketing card.

A client's research card from your contact client list and his marketing card can be stapled or clipped together to keep all information in one place.

With either form of contact, reminder mailings should be sent, depending on finances, every six weeks to three months. A *reminder*, which can be a flyer or mailer, puts your name and work in front of the client's eyes to refresh his/her memory. You can also use these mailings to announce an award, an exhibition, or a change in medium or style. Send them to clients who expressed interest but couldn't handle or buy your work at the time.

Flyers and mailers used as reminder mailings should always contain fresh images. Update each mailing to the same clients or have a series of reminders printed simultaneously and mail a new image from the series. Usually three to four reminder mailings are sufficient (depending on the time span). After this, either submit new samples, call for another review if you want to pursue the client, or drop the name from your active mailing list.

Maintain marketing cards on booth shows and competitions as well. If your filing system allows, staple the card directly to the prospectus; otherwise, maintain a file for prospectuses and another for the cards. As with interviews and mailings, list all pertinent information: name of show, contact person, address, phone number. Follow with the date the prospectus was received, deadline dates, notification dates, and the action you take. If you enter the show, list the date and number of slides sent and the names of the paintings. Follow with whether your work was accepted or rejected, and any further action, such as the date works were shipped, names of works shipped, and so on. If not entering the show, briefly note why.

Let your daily calendar and marketing cards work hand in hand; your efforts then remain organized and efficient. The time you spend updating the cards and marking the calendar will be made up by clearing your mind for art, freeing you from the worry of forgetting an appointment or a deadline, or wondering when you did your last mailing. Your marketing cards further work for you by tracking changes within businesses, especially addresses and contact persons. You know your status with each potential client. Not only are your records up-to-date, but soon, with an overview of each potential client, you can spot the gallery that's changed ownership several times in one year or the show that can't find its focus. These serve as red flags—drop them from your active client list.

APPROACHING THE CLIENT

Potential clients are approached in two ways: in person and through the mail. Your clients' locations and your individual sales personality and time restrictions dictate whether you make client contact through in-person reviews or through mail submissions. Each method has its unique advantages.

With in-person interviews, you know for certain that the potential client is really reviewing your work—it hasn't been put aside to gather dust in a corner. You have the opportunity to ask and answer questions, add verbal details about your work and talent, and give specifics about why your artwork is appropriate for and beneficial to this client. You receive instant feedback regarding your artwork; you can "read" facial expressions and body language, and ask for the client's professional opinion.

Mail submissions allow you to contact numerous potential clients at one time, to have your work seen simultaneously nationwide. You save time and money because, once the mailing package is planned, all duplicates and printing can be accomplished at once and you can collate packages in assembly-line fashion.

If you're a part-time artist who isn't able to meet with art clients during regular business hours, mailing packages can be put together and sent out in the evenings and over weekends. With mailed submissions, you're able to initiate client contact when *you* have the time, not according to the client's schedule.

Organization and preparation are vital to

both types of contact. It is important to approach the client with as much knowledge as possible.

The In-person Interview

Everyone gets nervous going to interviews, but it becomes easier the more you do it. The better prepared you are, the greater your comfort. The challenge is to arrive at each interview prepared to show examples of your work geared to the needs of the outlet.

Gallery directors, shop owners, or graphic arts buyers are people with businesses to run, ringing telephones, bills to pay, time schedules, and sixty other people wanting their attention. What do these clients want from you? They want to briefly meet you personally, then see your artwork presented in a clear manner to quickly establish what you do and how well you do it. If the client believes your work fits into current or future plans, she will further explore your experience to better judge your commitment to art and career achievement. Lastly, the client wants something on hand as a reminder of your work and how to reach you. Your portfolio and printed marketing tools must meet all these requirements.

Some basic business protocol must be followed when setting interviews.

Always make an appointment. No matter how large or small the potential client's business, the director/owner cannot stop everything to see you because you "happened to be in the area and thought you'd drop by." It happens, yes, but it's not likely to happen. In business, everyone lives on a schedule, and an appointment is your way of grabbing a piece of this person's business day. Besides, you want the director/owner's attention on your work and, if he's expecting you, presumably he carves time out *only* for you.

When phoning for an appointment, speak slowly and distinctly, immediately stating your name and reason for calling. Be friendly and courteous to the person answering the phone; you might be speaking with the very person who later reviews your work. If you don't know the name of the person who reviews work, ask. Write that name down on your 3″x5″ marketing card and request a review.

If several days intervene between your phone call and the actual appointment, call the day before to confirm. Schedules go topsy-turvy even in the most organized situations, and a needless trip can be avoided. If the director/owner postpones and reschedules, keep in mind that this is better than a rushed review overshadowed by other issues. If *you* can't make the appointment, phone and reschedule.

Arrive a few minutes before the scheduled hour and dress according to the business standards of your community. You are there to conduct business and that's the image to convey.

When you actually meet the client, offer a firm handshake and direct eye contact. Even if you're apprehensive, appear as if you possess confidence in yourself and in your work. When you believe your work is good, that belief is expressed without words in everything you do.

Have all business materials at your fingertips. Bring a small portfolio of slides or photographs (or small original works), printed marketing materials and a leave-behind packet. *Don't* arrive weighted down with large, awkward cases or numerous cardboard tubes of rolled works. You'll appear overwhelming and disorganized. If you're bringing large original works, place them in a manageable portfolio case and, immediately upon arrival, set this case discreetly out of the way. Or leave large original works in your locked car. You won't show these unless the director/owner asks to see them.

Your slide/photograph portfolio should fit comfortably on the client's desk and its review should take place without another word from you. Your information sheet (if present) can either be at the front of the portfolio and mentioned, or handed directly to the reviewer. If the owner/director is interested enough to go through the portfolio to the end, a resume can be placed here (either loose or in a protective sheet) so that she can immediately move to reviewing your background and experience.

Questions are bound to be asked. Some clients ask first, then look; others ask while they're looking; still others wait until they're finished reviewing your work. Take your cue from the client; don't be distracting with superfluous comments just because you're nervous.

If your portfolio is in slides, find out beforehand if the client has viewing facilities. Even so, carry a small hand-held viewer to appointments "just in case." Hand viewers are not expensive; many are battery operated, providing a back light and a small magnifying screen.

The physical arrangement of the office or facility may dictate how much of a role you play in the slide viewing, but generally speaking, stand or sit in the background. Usually you'll be able to give verbal descriptions during the viewing; if the director/owner doesn't want this, then have your information sheet available for her to read. Some clients will place your slides on a light table and quickly scan them, selecting only a few to view blown up. While this is disappointing, be encouraged that she was interested enough to select some. Some clients will use only the light table with no magnification; this is frustrating because you know much of the impact and detail to your work isn't being seen; offer your hand viewer.

Once the interview is over (take your cue from the client), express how much you'd like her to handle your work and state the reasons why. Present your leave-behind packet. Only in situations where there's absolutely no interest in your work should you not leave materials with the client. Even then there's a temptation to leave some anyway—it never hurts to be on file.

When you get home, fill out the client's marketing card with the pertinent information: date of interview, impressions, type of presentation, the materials you left behind, type of follow-up planned, and results of the interview.

If you're offered a contract on the spot, don't panic. Sometimes we're so tuned in to rejection or noncommitment that, when an offer arrives, we turn to jelly.

If the client offers to sell or handle your work, listen carefully to what he/she is saying. Take notes (pack a pad and pencil in your case). You want to compare what the director/owner is verbally promising to what is actually printed in the contract. If the shop/gallery doesn't offer a pre-printed contract, you want a solid foundation of agreement on which to base the written contract you'll present. Do not sign a contract at this time; take the opportunity to read and study it under less stressful conditions. You might want a lawyer with expertise in handling contracts for creative people to read it. Express your pleasure in being offered the opportunity to work with this client and request twenty-four hours in which to go over the contract and give your answer. And honor the time request; don't leave the client hanging.

Once you go over the contract, a point or phrase may not be clear to you. Call the client immediately for clarification. If there are unacceptable clauses, remember that contracts are negotiable and can be rewritten. Negotiation is an acquired art. A mutually satisfactory agreement is your goal; neither party should be out to win at all costs. The only way the client is going to know your needs and wants is for you to tell him. Know the extent to which you will compromise; don't totally capitulate just to get the contract or sale. For example, if a gallery seeks exclusive representation of your work for the entire city and this cuts deeply into your sales, ask the reason behind the request. Explain how this affects your current finances and sales. Suggest alternative solutions and listen to the client's ideas until you reach an agreement you both can live with comfortably. By negotiating with patience rather than anger, you'll be known as an artist who's easy to work with, yet very professional and businesslike.

No one can predict exactly how each interview will be conducted because no two situations are exactly alike. But if you treat each person with respect, believe in your art and in your business abilities, and fully prepare for each review, you'll emerge a winner.

Use interviews as learning situations. Analyze each of them to determine what you could have done differently or which materials might have better served you. If you feel you did everything right and still did not get a contract or sale, then it simply means your work wasn't what this client needed at this time.

The Mailed Art Submission

When you contact clients through the mail, your mailing package takes on the role you and your work performed at the in-person interview. Thus, your highest priority is to make it *communicate*—visually through the design of your enclosures and work samples, and verbally through your cover letter and the written texts on your marketing tools.

A cover letter is a sales pitch—your chance to state the who, what, why, where, when, and how of you and your art.

Who and What: Who you are and what you do. Use descriptive language, just as you did on your letterhead and business card, but more so. Instead of saying you're an artist, tell what kind of an artist you are and what type of art you specialize in. Gear your descriptions to the client or market area you're approaching.

Why and Where: Why you'd like the client to handle or sell your work. Highlight your strongest personal points as well as those of your work. If you're familiar with a positive aspect of the client's business or product, incorporate it into your letter—everyone likes praise. For example, note how a gallery's effective use of greenery and spot-lighting creates a restful atmosphere for a visitor while artfully highlighting an artist's work.

The *where* is a brief listing of where you've sold your work before (a mini-list of clients specifically of interest to your potential client) or where your work has been exhibited or won awards. If you don't have any of these credits, ignore this.

When and How: These two are combined to wind up the letter, either by stating when and how you can be contacted or when and how you plan a follow-up to your package. You can also state what action you'd like the potential client to take with your package—file it for future reference, return your samples to you in the enclosed SASE, or retain some samples and return the others.

The cover letter should never be longer than one page, typed on your letterhead. Always address your letter and mailing package to a specific person even if it means a brief long-distance phone call to the business to learn the

HOW TO PREPARE FOR A GALLERY REVIEW

When New Mexico artist Michaellallen McGuire goes to a gallery review, he prepares for any situation that might arise. He admits that he tries to cover all bases so that no matter what a gallery director should ask for, he'll have it with him. "I try to have photographs, 4″ × 6″s, 5″ × 7″s, or 8″ × 10″s. The problem is that you can't get perfectly color-accurate photographs."

So McGuire brings slide sheets and an Agfa loupe. "You can hold it up and look at the painting in great detail." He also carries a portable slide projector. "I have a second separate set of slides identical to those in the slide sheet. If the gallery director doesn't like the slide sheet and complains, I can immediately set up the slide projector. I run through the same slides on a viewing mechanism that enlarges them. If the director's not satisfied with any of these, then I can't help him out. Generally one of these things does the job."

McGuire follows other business protocol. "I always call ahead and make an appointment and carry bio material, pricing information, and a list of pieces available for sale. I try to get as much information across as I can in as little time as possible."

When soliciting through the mail, he sends a complete package. "The slide sheet goes out, photographs go with it, an inventory sheet, a list of pieces available for sale, a resume, short bio sheet, a cover letter explaining what I'm after, an explanation of prices, a business card, a photograph of myself, and an SASE, stamped and ready to go. I make it as easy for the client as possible.

"I always want my slides returned, because they're infinitely more valuable to me than to the client, but I always have photographs the client can keep on hand with the cover letter, etc."

appropriate person's name. Check for correct spelling of the name, and, in some cases, verify whether male or female—names can be deceiving.

The other enclosures should be visually unified and convey as much information as possible. Include a brochure or a flyer-mailer-resume combination. A business card is optional, but include it if other printed pieces don't carry address/phone information.

The types of samples you send depend on whether your work is in black and white or color and whether you expect their return. If you work in color, enclose slides or photographs. Slides should be in a plastic slide sheet cut to accommodate the number of slides. Photographs can be held together in clear acetate cover sheets and a plastic slip-on spine. All of your materials can be placed in a two-pocket folder. *Just be certain your final product fits an 8½"x11" file drawer.* If you don't want your samples returned, three to five are sufficient. If you want them returned send as many as fifteen to twenty to give the client a broader selection. Beyond twenty is overkill. Consider the mailing weight and cost of each package, and decide whether you're giving the client fresh images with each sample or merely trying to impress with quantity. And remember that samples might not be returned even if you request their return and enclose an SASE.

If you work in black and white, mail less expensive black-and-white photographs, photostats, or photocopies and don't request a return. You might not want to invest in the extra cost for slides and color photographs of black-and-white work; make them a choice only if the other three sample types don't do your work justice.

Do not send your entire portfolio, original work, or tearsheets (unless you have hundreds). The likelihood of these samples getting lost, mislaid, or not returned is too great. The only exception to this is a specific request from the director/owner for these items. Even then, if you're not comfortable, don't risk your whole portfolio.

For added protection during mailing, invest in "bubble" envelopes (inside protection is a sheet of plastic filled with air bubbles), envelopes lined with a thin sheet of styrofoam, or extra-strength envelopes. These cost more but survive mailing virtually unscathed. Buying envelopes in bulk saves money. Place sufficient postage on the SASE for the weight of the return package.

If you're including a reinforced return envelope, you probably will not be able to fold it. You'll need to buy two envelope sizes, one the correct size for returning the samples, the other large enough to accommodate the full size of the smaller envelope and the mailing package.

A free booklet, *A Consumer's Directory of Postal Services and Products*, is available at your local post office or by writing Consumer Advocate, U.S. Postal Service, Washington, D.C. 20260-6320. This booklet provides information on the mail services offered by the U.S. Postal Service; proper addressing and packaging; special services, such as insurance, claims, special delivery and certified mail; military mail; and international mail, mail fraud and mail problems; and other services, such as postage meters, passport applications, and self-service postal centers. Armed with this knowledge, you can select the services most appropriate to your mailing needs, whether business or personal, and know what to do if a problem arises.

When addressing your mailing package, address only one side of the envelope, be sure your return address is in the upper-left corner, and don't decorate it with cutesy stamps or dire handwritten warnings. Writing "First Class" or "Do Not Fold" once is sufficient; better yet, ask the postal attendant to stamp it when you mail it or buy your own stamp. Be sure to include the addressee's zip code; the post office suggests that, for the best possible service, capitalize everything in the address, eliminate all punctuation and use the two-letter state abbreviations.

First class is the fastest mail class for your mailing package if it weighs twelve ounces or less; if it isn't letter size, be sure it's marked first class or use a green-bordered large envelope.

Priority mail is first-class mail that weighs more than twelve ounces and less than seventy pounds. It receives the same two- to three-day service as first class. Free priority mail stickers are available from your local post office.

Second-class mailing is available only to publishers and registered news agents who have the authorized privilege of mailing at second-class pound rates.

Third-class mail is often referred to as bulk business mail, but it can be used by anyone since there are two rate structures: one for a single piece and one for bulk mail. Your parcel must weigh less than sixteen ounces. Frequently the difference in postal costs between priority mail and third class is only a matter of a nickel or dime and it's worth the faster service to go with priority mail. If you're doing a large mailing, however, consider third class since the nickels and dimes can add up. Contact your local post office for further information on the regulations governing a bulk mailing.

Fourth class (parcel post) is for packages weighing from one to seventy pounds, but is the slowest of the postal services. Unless the price difference is exorbitant, consider using priority mail instead.

It's tempting to think you need more postal service than you really do when you're mailing out packages that mean so much to your career. Some artists feel more attention will be paid to their package if it's sent special delivery, registered mail or Express Mail. Probably not. Consider special mail services for sending original art, but not samples.

There are some items you can request from the post office that are helpful to you. Always ask for a cash receipt for your record-keeping and as proof to the IRS should you be audited.

For a fee you can request a certificate of mailing, a receipt that shows evidence of mailing (not that the package was received, but that you mailed it). No record of the mailing is kept at the post office. This certificate is especially important when returning signed contracts; a contract is valid once it has been mailed even if the other party doesn't receive it.

Certified mail, available only for first-class pieces, provides you with a mailing receipt and a record of delivery is maintained at the recipient's post office. For an additional fee you can request a return receipt which provides you with proof of delivery.

United Parcel Service (UPS) accepts packages up to fifty pounds and, besides its regular service, offers a two-day air service and a next-day service in some areas. Numerous overnight air-freight services also abound, but these aren't really necessary for sample packages. Check into UPS services if you'll be mailing large packages or into overnight services for competition/show entry slides when meeting a tight deadline. All are willing to give rate and restriction information over the phone and have brochures outlining their services.

UPDATING YOUR MARKETING STRATEGY

As six months or so go by (depending on the scope and frequency of your marketing endeavors), take stock of where you are and where you're heading. Some surprising changes might have occurred that require re-evaluating your marketing tools and marketing field. You might find yourself selling in an area you hadn't anticipated when you began. Perhaps an architect approached you to supply artwork for his new office building and he recommended you to another; your sales are now through architects and interior designers, though you'd started out marketing to galleries. Or the fields you first approached aren't supplying you with enough sales to keep you at the standard of living you seek. Or you're finding success locally while most of your marketing efforts were nationwide. Or you simply need some fresh images in your marketing materials and portfolio.

Careers evolve, and what was right for you six months ago might not be right for you today. Set aside a day (yes, mark it on your calendar) to look over your portfolio, marketing tools, and index cards. Think hard about your current situation, and list what you like and dislike about it. How can you change the negatives? A different field, better market research, better pricing standards? Perhaps you need more schooling to increase skills or a more thorough understanding of business concepts. Would membership in an artists' organization help?

Review your marketing tools:

- Does your resume need updating so current sales, collections, commissions, awards, and exhibitions are listed?
- Does the artwork on your brochure look outdated?
- Does the written text reflect your current artistic and professional image?
- Would you enjoy a new look to your stationery and business card?
- Have you moved or changed your phone number?

Go through your index file. Delete cards over a year old from which you've had no response. Enough money's been spent on them. Review the ones left—do they spark any new ideas? Seeing your successes and failures in black and white clarifies why you've been successful with some clients and not others.

Now is also the time to ask yourself how you feel about your art career as a whole. Do you still feel mentally, physically, and emotionally good about it? If not, is it time to evaluate and update your overall lifestyle? Should you consider fine art part-time while bringing in a steady income from another source, or vice versa—drop full-time employment to devote more time to your fine art career?

When you've decided what you need to freshen your marketing approach and professional outlook, go back to square one and proceed just as you did in the beginning. Your short-range goals might once again include printers' price quotes and reproduction of your work. Your long-range goal might be to set up appointments with potential clients in an untried field.

Reserve specific times for reevaluation to keep your career fresh and growing. There is never a time to quit marketing. The form of marketing might change as you become more successful and gallery directors and interior designers seek you instead of the other way around. But even noted artists rely on marketing to reach their consumers.

CHAPTER FIVE
CHECKLISTS

To initiate a marketing plan:
- [ ] Determine whether contact is in-person, by mail, or both
- [ ] Allocate most money to your best samples
- [ ] Budget and plan for follow-up mailings
- [ ] Understand your needs
- [ ] Know the demands of the market area you're approaching
- [ ] Focus materials to clients' interests
- [ ] Develop multi-purpose printed tools
- [ ] Know that no single piece meets all communication needs

To organize your marketing efforts:
- [ ] Develop a marketing calendar to track appointments, deadlines, goals
- [ ] Use 3″ × 5″ index cards for specific client marketing activity
- [ ] Record dates and results of mailings and interviews on cards
- [ ] Utilize a master card for listing package and leave-behind contents

For an effective in-person review:
- [ ] Always make an appointment
- [ ] Confirm appointment the day before
- [ ] Prepare materials beforehand
- [ ] Edit portfolio to meet client's interest
- [ ] Dress according to prevailing business standards
- [ ] Offer firm handshake and direct eye contact
- [ ] Bring small portfolio of slides and/or photographs

- [ ] Bring printed marketing materials and prepared leave-behind packet
- [ ] Include hand-held viewer and original works (optional)
- [ ] Answer questions as asked; don't interrupt review with comments
- [ ] Take cue from reviewer regarding end of interview
- [ ] Present leave-behind packet once review ends
- [ ] Complete client's marketing card at home
- [ ] Set date for follow-up mailing on card and calendar

The mailed submission:
- [ ] Can be tailored to specific region or type of market
- [ ] Often receives no reply
- [ ] Doesn't allow you to discuss work face-to-face with reviewer
- [ ] Must be sent to specific contact person
- [ ] Should contain three to five slides or photographs
- [ ] Never send portfolio or original work
- [ ] Enclose SASE for return of samples (optional)

A good cover letter is:
- [ ] One page
- [ ] Typed on letterhead
- [ ] Covers who you are, what you do, why you're writing, and when and how you can be contacted

CHAPTER 6

THE BUSINESS
OF ART

BUSINESS REGULATIONS FOR THE SELF-EMPLOYED

As a self-employed businessperson, you must be familiar with the regulations governing your business operation. You are responsible to local, state, and federal governments, and it's *your* responsibility to find out the exact regulations.

Local regulations differ from city to city, so they can only be addressed in generalities here.

The most common procedure, if you're operating your business within a city's limits, is to register the business with the city offices. Cities usually require mandatory registration

■ They want to know what kinds of operations are being conducted within their limits.

■ It alerts city offices to business operations that might be illegal or require further licensing, such as those handling hazardous wastes or those involving health care.

■ It gives city offices the opportunity to check the zoning status of the area where the business is being operated. If yours is a home-based business, it is probably zoned residential, which usually means restrictions on noise, traffic, signs, and advertising.

■ Business registration also allows cities to claim their fair share of certain revenues from the state. A registration fee will probably be required from you by the city.

If you live outside the city limits, you might be governed instead by county regulations. These might be similar to, but less restrictive than, city laws.

Most states today apply a sales tax or gross receipts tax to all businesses operating within the state. Upon registering your business with your city or county, you will probably be directed immediately to file as a business owner with your state revenue and taxation department. With this filing, you receive a tax identification number, important when selling your work or buying art materials. Depending on where you live, this number might have a different name: resale number, wholesale number, vendor number, or ID number. They all mean the same—the number that is assigned to your business license or certificate. This is the number state officials request at booth shows to confirm you're registered and paying the appropriate tax on your sales. It also allows you to buy art supplies either wholesale or without paying sales tax from certain outlets.

Once you've filed with the state and received your tax identification number, you're responsible for filing tax returns with the state. Depending on the amount of your taxable sales, you will file on a monthly, quarterly, or semi-annual basis. Some states require you to file a sales tax return even if you've made no sales at all. Some require sales tax payment only on sales actually made within the state; others want taxes paid on *all* sales. State laws vary widely, so check into this aspect of your tax liability very carefully. Otherwise you might face fines or back taxes plus interest.

Where do you find this vital information? First call your city or county clerk's office. If this office isn't available to you, call the local office of your state's taxation and revenue department. In some large cities, there's a "How-to-Register-Your-Business" listing in the blue pages of the telephone book, a recorded message supplying all registration information. If none of these sources yield the information you need, go to any small business in your area and ask the owner where and how his or her business license was obtained.

In addition to sales or gross receipts tax, some states also have state income tax—a tax normally filed at the same time as you file your federal income tax. This tax is totally separate from any sales tax. If you've already been filing state income tax because of a spouse's income or a previous occupation, these forms are probably sent to your home automatically. If not, check with your state tax department to find out what forms you need and when they are to be filed.

FEDERAL TAXES

The final tax agency you are responsible to as a self-employed businessperson is the federal government, the Internal Revenue Service.

The federal government is interested in your business because the money earned from your artwork is income and, depending on the amount and how you're filing, can be taxable.

You are now responsible for filing a "Schedule C—Profit or (Loss) from Business or Profession" with your other income tax forms.

The attitude of the IRS toward creative self-employed businesspersons is relatively straightforward; that is, you are responsible for keeping track of all business-related expenses and income. If your legitimate expenses are greater than your income, you have operated your business at a *loss*, and this loss may be used to reduce your total taxable income. If you have made a profit, you are responsible for paying income tax on that money.

Especially for fine artists, the IRS has as its main concern whether you are actually carrying on a business or merely pursuing art as a hobby. If you are a business, you have the opportunity to declare those business losses in years you don't have art income exceeding expenses. If the IRS determines your art is only a hobby, however, your deductions can only *equal* the amount of income made from your art—you can't operate a hobby at a loss and reduce other taxable income.

How does the IRS make this distinction? By looking at your profit motive. Obviously the easiest way for a self-employed businessperson to prove profit motive is to make a profit, so the IRS has determined that if the "business activity" makes a profit any three out of five consecutive years, it has profit motive and is indeed a business, not a hobby.

If, however, you do not show a profit, you can face a "hobby challenge" by the IRS. If the IRS proves its claim of a hobby status regarding your activity, some prior deductions can be declared invalid and you're liable for back taxes. But you also have the opportunity to show that, in spite of not making a profit, you are indeed conducting a business or trade and are trying to make a profit.

The regulations of the Internal Revenue Code are the objective standard by which the IRS judges profit motive. Nine factors are listed so that all circumstances surrounding an activity can be used to determine its status, and no single factor outweighs the others. Knowledge of these factors will provide you with further information regarding what are considered acceptable business criteria. The IRS reviews:

- The manner in which you conduct business, that is, accuracy of record-keeping, possession of receipts, etc. Ownership of marketing and promotional materials also help to show an intent to sell.
- The expertise of you and your advisors. This includes study, peer and professional acceptance through awards, exhibitions, professional memberships; knowledge and use of professional equipment and techniques.
- Time and effort expended on art activity. The IRS doesn't demand that you pursue art full-time, but is more concerned that sufficient consistent time and effort are expended to make a profit possible.
- The expectation that your artworks will increase in value. This criterion is usually not applied to the arts because all artists anticipate that their work will increase in value.
- Your success in previously attempted business activities. If you were successful before and are simply experiencing a slack period, this counts in your favor.
- Your history of art income or losses. If your income from art has increased slowly over the years in spite of never exceeding expenses, this is a factor in favor of profit motive.
- The amount of occasional profits you earn compared to the amount of the expenses. This factor is used primarily in situations where the taxpayer is sufficiently wealthy to be gaining significant tax reductions by operating an art career at a loss, yet is experiencing no severe financial strain from the expenses.
- Your financial status. Sad, but true, the IRS considers that the more destitute you

are, the greater your profit motive. If you are already wealthy or have an income independent of your art career, your profit motive is considered lessened.

- Elements of personal recreation or pleasure. This factor is usually applied primarily when travel is involved to further an art activity.

Rulings by the tax courts define and interpret tax laws, but, especially in these times of law changes, you need to keep as up-to-date as possible. The IRS has a free publication: Publication 334, "Tax Guide for Small Business." Two tax guides published yearly that contain tax forms as well as other detailed tax information are *Arthur Young Tax Book* and *J.K. Lasser's Your Income Tax*. Though not directed specifically to artists, these books give information for self-employed businesspersons. National art organizations and Volunteer Lawyers for the Arts, as well as other art lawyer organizations, offer workshops and booklets on artists' taxes.

RECORD-KEEPING

Accurate, consistent record-keeping is absolutely essential for good business. Not only do your records determine your legitimate expenses and deductions, but they detail your income, providing an overall picture of how well your business is or isn't doing. At the end of the year, look over your sales and determine which size, price range, and subject matter of your paintings sold best. Review your expenses; ascertain if equipment investments can reduce expenses, such as purchasing a home copier to reduce photocopying expenses. The picture is clearer when you see the figures in black and white.

Consider paying a professional accountant to set up your books the first time. Once you understand the entries, maintain the books yourself from then on.

If you wish to set up your own books, here's a suggested format. Look at the Schedule C tax form and find the headings the IRS uses for deductions. These include advertising, car and truck expenses, dues and publications, legal and professional services, office expense, rent,

repairs, utilities and telephone, and so on.

Buy a columnar book, either a self-contained style or one punched with holes fitting a three-ring notebook. The latter is extremely helpful because pages can be moved around, a blank page easily inserted behind one that has been filled. At the top of a page, place the year for which the records are being kept, whether expenses or income, and the specific category. For example, "1989 Expenses, Office Expense." Simply enter each expense under its appropriate category, providing as many specifics as possible.

Income also should be very detailed. When income is received, list the date, the nature of the income (sale of artwork, royalty, installment payment), title of the work, size, and medium of the piece (if applicable), and the name of person/company paying. If this was a sale on consignment through a gallery, list the retail price, the gallery's commission and the amount you actually received. This gives you a thorough record of financial dealings that is a valuable future reference.

Aside from this record book of expenses and income, it's also wise to keep an inventory of your works. This, in essence, is a history of each major work from its inception to the present. Either on index cards or in a notebook, record:

- The title of the work, size, medium, and date completed.
- A brief one-line description of subject matter.
- Copyright number (if registered).
- Brief description of and approximate cost of materials.
- Approximate time for completion.
- Its history—exhibitions; consignment; competitions, including awards and prizes; sale, including name of buyer, date, sale terms, price, commission paid (if any); publicity, including articles and reviews; reproduction, including prints and posters; insurance.

If possible, attach a photograph or slide of the work directly to its informational card/ sheet; if not possible, list what this visual docu-

MAINTAINING A RECORD BOOK

Columnar sheets punched to fit a three-ring notebook make this record book easy to maintain. New sheets can be inserted as the previous sheet fills. The second notebook holds pocket folder pages, each with a pocket to keep receipts in order by the month.

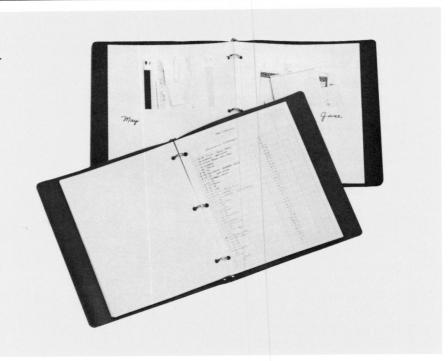

mentation is and where it's located.

This type of inventory takes time and effort, but is invaluable in documenting your works for insurance purposes or for the IRS. It helps to prove your seriousness as an artist and businessperson, and to validate the expenses incurred for each work.

Keeping Track of Receipts

It's mandatory to retain all receipts for art-related expenses, but keeping them organized until recorded is the hardest part. Not only do these slips of paper disappear, but remembering each purchase can be confusing, especially with cash register receipts that state only a price, not an itemized description.

Utilizing some tricks and developing buying habits minimize the confusion.

Buy either envelope-style or pocket folders from a local office supply or discount store. Pocket folders routinely have two pockets; envelope-style folders have anywhere from one pocket to expandable multiple pockets. Label each pocket for one month of the year. As you purchase art-related items, immediately place the receipt from that purchase into its appropriate monthly pocket. Record your purchases from these receipts into your expense record book bi-weekly or monthly, depending on the extent of your purchases. Once the purchases have been recorded, paper clip this stack of receipts. You can then transfer them to yet another folder marked with the year date or leave them in the monthly folder. Either way, at the end of the year, your receipts are in chronological order and at your fingertips.

To organize the purchases themselves on the receipt, develop the habit of carrying a pen and a highlighter marker pen. If you make an art-related purchase from a drugstore or discount store where the cash register receipt shows only prices (especially if it's among other purchases not related to art), immediately highlight the price that pertains to the art-related purchase. On the back of the receipt, with the pen, list by name the art-related items; even one-word item descriptions are enough to jog your memory when recording time arrives.

Whenever possible, pay for items by check or credit card. It's preferable to establish a checking account that is strictly for business. Again, this not only helps to show you as a serious business person, but also keeps household money separate from business money.

Logging Business Miles

Another necessary business habit is to write down your business mileage, that is, any art-related miles put on your car. Car expense is a legal deduction on your federal income tax, but you must be able to show a record of your actual mileage.

A small notebook carried either in your purse or the glove compartment suffices, though printed logs purchased from office supply or stationery stores provide specific headings for each bit of information. Some logs also have space for the trip's purpose and expenses, so they do double-duty as an aid to your expense recording.

CONTRACTS

Written contracts or agreements always protect you the most and help to avoid artist/client misunderstandings. By placing verbal promises and statements of fact in writing, both parties know exactly their duties, responsibilities, and rights. Written agreements increase your chance of winning a legal dispute; written proof carries more weight than verbal statements.

Contracts vary according to each situation; change them to suit your needs. Rely on pre-contract negotiations to form the base for your written contract. Do as much negotiating as possible in writing—use letters to confirm verbal phone conversations and letters of agreement to suggest terms, for example. With this written material on hand, drawing up the final contract is greatly simplified.

You don't have to have an attorney to write your contract. If you and your client have agreed to fair terms, the contract can be typed up at home on either plain paper or letterhead. Two copies of any agreement should exist; both you and the other party sign both copies. Keep one copy in your files. If you are working through the mail, and are initiating the contract, sign both copies, mail both to the other party for signing, and request that one signed copy be returned to you. Keep a third copy for your records until the signed copy is returned.

If you are photocopying an agreement, sign both copies *after* photocopying so that all signatures are original.

The contracts presented in this chapter are accompanied by point-by-point explanations. Read the contract and its explanations together.

Bills of Sale

Every time you sell a work of art, a written record of the transaction should exist. Two types of bills of sale are presented here—a long form and a short form. For the majority of sales, the short form suffices.

The Long Form. The long form (pages 94-95) focuses on the artwork's future use and allows the artist more control over the work's exhibition and treatment standards after sale.

Routinely, this contract begins with the names and addresses of the parties involved (titled Artist and Purchaser in the contract), followed immediately by a statement clarifying that the artist is the creator of the work and by a description of the work being sold.

1. This paragraph states the price at which the work is being sold to the purchaser. If installment payments are involved, spell out exactly how many payments are due, the amount of each, and the dates of commencement and completion.

2. Paragraph two acknowledges your interest in the future of your work and obligates the purchaser to notify you before placing the work in an exhibition. This allows you to know when and where your work is being seen. For more control over exhibition by the purchaser, further language must be added. A sample is: "Before committing Artwork to a show, Purchaser must notify Artist of intent to do so, supply to Artist all known details of the show, and receive Artist's written permission."

You can define your "paternity rights" here, that is, receive credit for your work by having your name identified with it. If you're selling to someone who apparently plans to display the work, require that display be accompanied by attribution. The contract phrase might read: "All public display of Artwork will include material identifying its artist as [your name]."

Agreement of Original Sale of Artwork

Artist: Purchaser:

    Name _____   Name _____

    Address _____   Address _____

    City State Zip _____   City State Zip _____

WHEREAS, Artist has created that certain Artwork:

Title: _____

Medium: _____

Dimensions: _____

Year of Completion: _____

and the parties mutually agree as follows:

1. SALE: Artist sells the Artwork to Purchaser at the agreed value of $ _____ .

2. PURCHASER EXHIBITION: Before committing the Artwork to a show, Purchaser must give Artist notice of intent to do so, telling Artist all details of the show that Purchaser knows.

3. PROVENANCE: Upon request, Artist will furnish Purchaser and his successors a written provenance and history of the Artwork based on Artist's best information.

4. ARTIST EXHIBITION: Artist may show the Artwork for up to sixty (60) days once every five (5) years at a nonprofit institution at no expense to Purchaser, upon written notice no later than one hundred twenty (120) days before opening and upon satisfactory proof of insurance and prepaid transportation.

5. NONDESTRUCTION: Purchaser will not permit any intentional destruction, damage, or modification of the Artwork.

6. RESTORATION: If the Artwork is damaged, Purchaser will consult Artist before any restoration is begun and must give Artist first opportunity to restore it if practicable.

7. RENTS: If the Artwork is rented, Purchaser must pay Artist fifty percent (50%) of the rents within thirty (30) days of receipt.

8. COPYRIGHT AND REPRODUCTION: The copyright to the Artwork and all reproduction rights are reserved by Artist.

9. NOTICE: Notice, in the form shown at the end of this contract, must be permanently affixed to the Artwork, warning that ownership, etc., are subject to this contract. If, however, a document represents the Artwork or is part of the Artwork, Notice must instead be a permanent part of that document.

10. MORAL RIGHT: Purchaser will not permit any use of Artist's name or misuse of Artwork which would reflect discredit on Artist's reputation or violate the spirit of the Artwork.

11. DURATION: This contract binds the parties, their heirs, and all their successors in interest, and all Purchaser's obligations are attached to the Artwork and go with ownership of the Artwork, all for the life of the Artist and Artist's surviving spouse plus twenty-one (21) years. Exception: the obligation of Paragraphs Two (2), Three (3), Four (4), and Six (6) will last only for the Artist's lifetime.

12. ATTORNEY'S FEES: In any proceeding to enforce any part of this contract, the aggrieved party will be entitled to reasonable attorney fees in addition to any available remedy.

13. Unless otherwise noted, Artwork was received by Purchaser in perfect condition.

_____   _____
(Artist signature)   Date

_____   _____
(Purchaser signature)   Date

NOTICE

Ownership, transfer, exhibition, and reproduction of this Artwork are subject to a certain Contract dated _____ between:

Artist _____

Address _____

and

Purchaser _____

Address _____

Artist has a copy.

3. Here you agree to provide the purchaser and his/her successors with the origins and history of the work upon request.

4. This paragraph gives you the right to borrow your work for exhibition even though it is sold, but restricts the length of time and the type of exhibition site.

5. This information is important, because many purchasers believe ownership means they can do whatever they want to a painting. This clause clarifies your right not to have your work changed or damaged. You can also include that you'll provide the purchaser with a complete artwork maintenance description upon request.

6. Who knows the materials and methods of painting better than you? Paragraph six gives you the first opportunity to repair and restore the artwork should it be damaged. If this isn't possible, you are at least to be consulted before any restoration takes place.

7. The rental stipulations of paragraph seven allow you to share in revenues the purchaser might receive from the work.

8. Copyright ownership and reproduction rights are clarified here. You might also add that if the purchaser desires to reproduce the work, your written permission must be obtained first.

9. This clause brings to the purchaser's attention that the Notice at the bottom of the agreement is to remain attached to the work. Before you deliver the work to the purchaser, cut or copy the Notice from one copy of the agreement and attach it to the work. If there is absolutely no place for the Notice on the work, you should provide an additional document that describes the work and contains your signature, and attach the Notice to this document. This document should always be transferred as a legal part of the work. The Notice alerts any owner of the work to the existence of the contract and the obligation to abide by the stipulations it contains.

10. This presents your moral right to preserve your reputation and the integrity of the artwork and the purchaser's obligation to cooperate in the preservation.

11. This paragraph broadens the power of the contract beyond the death of either party and defines the duration of the contract.

12. This stipulates the payment of attorney's fees should a legal dispute arise.

13. This final point acknowledges the fact that the artwork was received in perfect condition, which prevents later claims of artist/transit damage.

Both parties must sign and date the agreement and, as usual, one copy remains with the artist and one with the purchaser.

Other points that can be included in this contract as additional clauses are:

- A request that a notice of change of address by either party be provided to the other party prior to the change.
- A statement that you have access to photograph the artwork at no expense to the purchaser.
- A stipulation that the purchaser have a first option to purchase future works, if agreeable to both parties.
- A clear description of the work. If this is a work in a series, this avoids any future confusion.
- Transportation costs and who pays them, especially if an out-of-town client is involved.

The Short Form. The short bill of sale (at right) is, in effect, a receipt. Its greatest advantage is that it states in writing that the copyright to the work and all its inherent reproduction rights are reserved by you, the artist. This clarifies to the buyer that you are aware of copyright, your ownership of the copyright, and that any unauthorized reproduction of the work violates your copyright. If the work is being sold to a person who is involved in the reproduction of artworks, it's wise to be even more clear by adding the phrase "Reproduction rights must be negotiated in a separate contract."

The short bill of sale is pretty straightforward. It begins with the artist's name, address, and phone number, along with the purchaser's similar data. A complete description of the work follows, including title, medium, size, and framing (if applicable). Next comes the

Bill of Sale

Artist: Purchaser:

    Name _____   Name _____

    Address _____   Address _____

    City State Zip _____   City State Zip _____

    Phone (   ) _____   Phone (   ) _____

Description of Artwork:

Purchase Price $ _____

Sales Tax $ _____

Delivery Charges $ _____

Balance Due $ _____

COPYRIGHT AND REPRODUCTION RIGHTS ARE RESERVED BY THE ARTIST.

_____   _____
(Artist signature)   Date

_____   _____
(Purchaser signature)   Date

purchase price, sales tax (if applicable), delivery charges (if any), and the balance due (if any). If a balance is due, the terms can be written in by hand; for example "Balance due in thirty (30) days," or "Balance due in two installments of $ _____ each, due on _____(date)_____ and ____(date)____ ."

Both parties sign the bill of sale and its duplicate. Besides providing an accurate sales record (invaluable for income tax record-keeping), duplicates will help you to develop a comprehensive mailing list and maintain a record of where your work is should you want to borrow it.

If your sales are numerous, such as at booth shows, consider having these bills of sale printed with carbon or carbonless duplication.

The Projansky Contract

The contract created by New York attorney Robert Projansky benefits you even more than the long bill of sale. It contains additional stipulations allowing the artist to collect a *resale royalty*.

A section of Projansky's expanded contract covers any re-transfer of the artwork from the current purchaser, whether through sale, trade, gift-giving, inheritance, or compensation for its destruction. The person receiving the money must pay you 15 percent of the *gross art profit* within thirty days and give you a Transfer Agreement and Record (TAR) properly filled out and signed by the new owner.

The TAR lists the actual sale price if the work is sold for money or the fair market value if the work is transferred in any other way. The *gross art profit* is the difference between the agreed value on the new TAR and the agreed value on the last prior TAR or on the original contract (if no prior resale has taken place), and is the amount on which the artist receives the royalty.

This section of the Projansky contract is not for everyone. Potential buyers resist it, and it's difficult to enforce the completion of TARs and payment of royalties. But the contractual provisions are available to you. To see a Transfer Agreement and Record, read the *Legal Guide for the Visual Artist* by Tad Crawford.

The Artist/Gallery Consignment Agreement

This consignment agreement (pages 99-100) deals with the consignment of only certain pieces to a gallery. This agreement is best used when you want the gallery to have control over only the works you decide to place, restricting its role in your artistic career.

Before any work is placed, discuss this contract with the gallery and make appropriate changes to the agreement. If the gallery has its own consignment agreement, review it before you place any work, and compare its points to these stated here.

1. The first paragraph confirms the gallery received your works *and* received them in perfect condition. This helps to allay any later allegation that damage to a painting was caused in transit from the artist and, therefore, is not the fault of the gallery.

If you're dealing with a gallery by mail, add a request for the return of one signed copy of this agreement.

2. The works that this agreement covers are listed and detailed so there is little chance of confusing which works are being consigned. If numerous works are being consigned, place this portion of the agreement on a separate sheet of paper and attach it to the agreement as Appendix A. In this case, your *first* paragraph can read: "You confirm receipt of my consigned artworks, in perfect condition unless otherwise noted, that are described in the Consignment Record, attached to this Agreement as Appendix A."

If your work is other than one-of-a-kind, two-dimensional paintings, you can include additional wording about prices and can change headings. Add that sales tax will be collected by the gallery and is not included in the specified retail price.

3. This statement specifies that the gallery has agency over (that is, acts as an agent for) only the described consigned works. This is important, because some galleries assume that if they are handling some of your works, they have the right to a commission on your other works, such as current projects or works sold from your studio. For added clar-

Artist/Gallery Consignment Agreement

Artist:

Name _____

Address _____

City State Zip _____

Phone (_____) _____

Gallery:

Representative's Name _____

Business Name _____

Address _____

City State Zip _____

Phone (_____) _____

WHEREAS, Artist wishes to have certain of his/her Artworks represented by Gallery and Gallery wishes to represent Artist, the parties mutually agree as follows:

1. RECEIPT OF ARTWORK: Gallery confirms receipt of Artist's consigned Artworks, in perfect condition unless otherwise noted.

2. CONSIGNMENT RECORD:

Title	Medium	Dimensions	Retail Price	Gallery Commission
1.				
2.				
3.				
4.				
5.				

3. SCOPE OF AGENCY: This agreement applies only to Artworks consigned under this Agreement and does not make Gallery a general agent for any other of Artist's artworks.

4. COPYRIGHT AND REPRODUCTION RIGHTS: Artist reserves the copyright and all reproduction rights to these consigned Artworks. Gallery will not permit any of the Artworks to be copied, photographed or reproduced without Artist's written permission. All approved reproductions will carry Artist's copyright notice: © 19___ _____. Gallery will print on each bill of sale: "The right to copy, photograph or reproduce the artwork(s) identified here is reserved by Artist, _____ ."

5. SALES: Upon sale of the Artwork(s), the retail price less Gallery's commission will be remitted to Artist within thirty (30) days after the sale. Title to these Artworks remains with Artist until the Artworks are sold and Artist is paid in full, at which time title passes directly to the purchaser.

6. LOSS/REMOVAL: Gallery assumes full responsibility for any consigned Artwork lost, stolen, or damaged while in Gallery's possession. Consigned Artworks may not be removed from Gallery's premises for purposes of rental, installment sales, or on approval with a potential purchaser without

Artist's permission. Artist may withdraw Artworks on thirty (30) days written notice. Gallery may return to Artist any of the consigned Artworks on thirty (30) days written notice.

7. TERMINATION: Consigned Artworks will be held in trust for Artist's benefit and will not be subject to claim by a creditor of Gallery. This Agreement terminates automatically upon Artist's death, or if Gallery becomes bankrupt or insolvent. Either party may terminate this Agreement by giving sixty (60) days notice in writing to the other party. Upon termination, all of Artist's consigned Artworks will be returned to Artist within thirty (30) days at Gallery's expense and all accounts settled.

_____   _____
(Artist signature)   Date

_____   _____
(Gallery Representative signature)   Date

_____
(Gallery Business Name)

ity, add a statement that you're free to exhibit and sell any work not consigned to the gallery under this agreement and that the gallery is not to receive a commission on any works sold except those described in the agreement. To inform the gallery that you're aware of its business situation, include a statement that you'll keep the gallery informed of any other agents representing your work.

If a gallery requests agency over some or all of your other works, state in writing *exactly* which works these are. For example, agency over all new works created after a specific date or only works in a particular medium? Who chooses which works go into the gallery? Does the gallery get a commission on studio sales? A sample statement is: "This Agréement applies only to the works described herein (or on the Consignment Record attached as Appendix A) and to all new works created by the Artist after [date] in the following media [list of media] which shall be selected by [artist or gallery], except those reserved for the artist's private collection."

4. This copyright information spells out that the copyright and all inherent reproduction rights reside with you. If the gallery wants to reproduce your work for any reason, such as for publicity, it must obtain your permission first. Some galleries request a blanket provision giving them the right to reproduce your work for advertising and publicity purposes. Before agreeing to this provision, know exactly how the gallery defines "publicity and advertising." Get in writing the parameters of these terms.

The next sentence presents the proper form of your copyright notice; your notice is to appear with each reproduction. The request for placement of your notice on bills of sale informs purchasers that they cannot reproduce your work without your permission. An alternative is to include the statement that you want only *your* bill of sale used for purchases of your work. Of course, be prepared to supply it to the gallery.

If the gallery wants the power to sell some specific reproduction rights, additional language must be added. You can allow the gallery this latitude, but include here that you want to

be notified before the sale takes place and the gallery must receive your written permission/approval for the sale. Clarify that the gallery won't receive commissions on royalties or sales of reproduction rights unless it handled or arranged the sale, in which case its sales commission is a stated, agreed upon percentage. A statement regarding when your commission is due you (30 days, etc.) should be present.

5. This paragraph specifies when you are paid for a work that is sold. The time limit stated in this agreement (thirty days) is preferable, but many galleries won't agree. Some have already established pay periods, such as the end of the month following the sale, sixty days, or within thirty days after the purchaser's check clears. But by starting with a time span of your preference, you at least facilitate dialogue on the subject. The second part of this paragraph clarifies the fact that you are the artwork's owner until a purchaser pays for it in full; then he becomes the new owner. This helps to establish you as the owner of the work and might aid in preventing the creditors of a bankrupt gallery from taking your consigned work as a gallery's assets.

If the gallery permits installment sales, specify how payment is to be made on these sales. Clarify that the gallery will apply the proceeds from the sale to pay you first. Once you are paid in full, then the gallery can collect its commission from the payments. Include a statement regarding when the payment is due you and insert a provision that the gallery agrees to guarantee the credit of its customers and to bear all losses due to a customer's credit failure.

If you're responsible for making payments to the gallery (studio sales, etc.), include specifics about when you will make payment. If you're handling installment payments, stipulate that the installments will pay *your* share first and then the gallery will receive its commission.

You might want to include a point about the gallery not changing the retail price; this means the gallery cannot offer discounts to anyone without your permission. If a gallery wants to offer trade discounts, a clause needs to be added stating that the gallery has the right to make the customary trade discounts not to exceed a certain percentage of the retail price without your written permission and that the discount will be subtracted from the gallery's commission, not from your share of the proceeds.

6. This paragraph covers several important points and is restrictive in your favor. The first point is that the gallery assumes full responsibility for the care of the work while in its possession. The next sentence says that the works cannot be removed from the premises without your permission. If you anticipate frequent removal (rentals, for example), insert the statement that the gallery will be responsible for your works whether they are on the gallery's premises, on loan, on approval, or otherwise removed. The next statement gives you an out should you need to borrow your works for a show; the gallery also has the right to return works to you.

Since no federal moral rights legislation has passed at the time of this writing, it's wise to state here that the gallery will not intentionally commit or authorize any physical defacement, mutilation, alteration, or destruction of any of your consigned works and will be responsible for cleaning, maintenance, and protection of the works. Include that you'll supply the gallery with a schedule of maintenance and, should damage occur, all repairs and restoration will have your written permission before being undertaken. You can request consultation prior to repair or restoration and be given first opportunity to accomplish the necessary work for a reasonable fee. If the artwork cannot be restored, and the damage is the fault of the gallery, stipulate that you will receive the same amount as if the work had been sold at the specified retail price with no deduction for a gallery commission. The damaged work is to be returned to you upon request.

7. This last paragraph is a further effort to prevent your works from being taken by the creditors of a bankrupt gallery. Frankly, these clauses don't always offer effective protection because the Uniform Commercial Code allows creditors to have rights against consigned goods. Twenty-one states *have* enacted con-

signment statutes that protect, to varying degrees, fine art from being taken by a gallery's creditors. Generally, under these consignment laws, the consigned works and the money from the sale of these works are held in trust for you and claims cannot be made against them by creditors. But these laws vary widely in their specific coverage and provisions, so it's best to contact either an attorney or the state legislature in the state in which the gallery is located to find out exactly what kind of protection the state has (if any) and what you need to do to give yourself maximum protection.

Having the agreement terminate if the gallery goes bankrupt or insolvent also offers some protection. Three steps you can take to help your cause are:

■ Have a *written* agreement, especially if the state has no consignment laws.
■ In your agreement make sure that you are established as the owner of the artworks.
■ Make it clear that these works are *consigned* to, not purchased by, the gallery by using the words "consignment" and "consigned" within your written agreement.

Add other termination considerations here, such as, termination if a trusted gallery employee dies or is fired, or if the gallery moves out of a specific geographical area; or a stipulation that the agreement cannot be terminated ninety days before or after a solo exhibition.

If you grant extensive exclusivity to the gallery or anticipate this gallery's representation to be a milestone in your career include:

■ The scope of the gallery's agency, that is, whether exclusive or nonexclusive and the geographical area and/or media covered.
■ The length of time the agreement is to be in effect.
■ A description of how you expect the gallery to give you continuous sales representation, promotion, and marketing.
■ A requirement of at least one solo exhibition during the term of the agreement and clarification of financial responsibilities, artistic control, artist notification, and di-

vision of post-exhibition property.
- A statement of gallery commissions on other income, such as rental fees, commissions to create artwork, prizes and awards, lecture fees, studio sales, etc.
- A statement of financial responsibility for delivery of works from artist to gallery, gallery to artist, and gallery to purchaser.
- Complete instructions regarding works removed from the gallery's premises for the purpose of rental, lending, installment sales, or on approval.
- A requirement that the gallery will keep accurate records and give you an accounting, including specifics on what that accounting entails.
- A statement that disputes will go to arbitration, including the name of the agreed-upon arbitrator.
- A statement that the agreement cannot be assigned or transferred without written consent, and requirement of artist notification regarding key personnel changes or gallery ownership change.
- A statement that modifications or changes to the agreement must be in writing and signed by both parties.
- A statement that the validity of the agreement is governed by the laws of a specified state.

COMMISSION AGREEMENTS

Artists faced with commissions must protect themselves from investing valuable time, money, and creative energy in a project that reaps no money. For this reason, the two-part commission agreement is recommended for your greatest protection. Most commissions fall apart due to client/artist miscommunication; these contracts establish open discussion and agreement of terms right from the beginning.

The commission agreement lessens your risk by staggering payment; at any point, should the client change his mind, each completed part of the design and final product has been paid for.

Before accepting a commission, be sure the client knows your style, medium, and technique. A client may commission a painting be-

cause she has heard you do good work, without seeing it firsthand. Insist that the prospective client view your work in your studio or at least review sharp, color-true slides or photographs. Your goal is for the client to be familiar and comfortable with the decision to give you the commission.

Once a client agrees that she likes your work, it's time to discuss the actual commission and to get the details in writing as an agreement.

All points in these contracts are negotiable and adjustable, to fit your situation. You can combine the two contracts if you wish but you're wiser to use two separate documents, especially for large, very expensive works.

The Commission Agreement for Design of Artwork

This agreement (pages 104-105) for the design of the commissioned work provides for understanding between you and the client. You are protected should the project be halted after the initial design because you have been paid for your time, creativity and product.

The agreement begins with the names and addresses of the two parties involved, the Collector and the Artist, and clarifies that the client is familiar with your work.

1. This section describes the project being commissioned (the anticipated finished product) and sets a price range for its completion. By not fixing an absolute price, you protect yourself against unanticipated time, complexity, or expense that might be unforeseen at this stage. Provide as detailed a description as possible, including subject matter (if applicable) and framing.

2. The first part of this section covers your fee for creating the design. This is a separate fee from the price of the final work, though some artists, if the client decides to go ahead with the project, subtract the design fee (which has already paid) from the final price. Whether you do depends entirely on your relationship with the client and your feelings about this practice. The next point informs the client when you will provide the preliminary design(s) and how long the client has to make a

Commission Agreement for Design of Artwork

Artist:

Name _____

Address _____

City State Zip _____

Phone (____) _____

Collector:

Name _____

Address _____

City State Zip _____

Phone (____) _____

WHEREAS, the Collector acknowledges sufficient familiarity with the style and quality of the work of the Artist, the parties mutually agree as follows:

1. DESCRIPTION: The Artist agrees to design (the Artwork) for an approximate production budget between $ _____ and $ _____. The Artwork is described as follows:

   Approximate size: _____

   Materials: _____

   Construction: _____

   Description: _____

2. DESIGN AGREEMENT: The receipt of good and valuable consideration of $ _____ on this day for the design work to be provided by Artist after signing of this Agreement is mutually acknowledged.

   A. Artist agrees to provide preliminary design of the Artwork to the Collector on or about ____(date)____.

   Upon receipt of the preliminary design, the Collector shall notify Artist within ten (10) days of any proposed changes in the preliminary design.

   B. Artist will provide a maximum of _____ designs or revisions for the Artwork. Additional designs or revisions shall cost an additional design fee of $ _____ per hour.

   C. If Collector decides to *not* proceed with creation of the Artwork, all designs must be returned to Artist. Artist shall retain the design fee, and this Agreement shall be terminated.

   D. If Collector decides to proceed with creation of the Artwork pursuant to a selected design, the Artwork Commission Agreement must be completed and signed by both parties, and the first one-third progress payment will be paid at that time.

3. EXPENSES: Collector is responsible for all expenses including, but not limited to, airfare and ground transportation, room and board, film and developing costs, shipping, insurance, and delivery charges. Artist will supply an itemized expense sheet including receipts.

4. COPYRIGHT: It is agreed that all designs are instruments of service and shall remain in the possession of and the property of the Artist. The Artist retains the exclusive right to use and create Artworks according to the designs. Collector agrees to make no public display or commercial use of the designs, or any copy or facsimile thereof, without the Artist's consent. It is agreed that if consent is granted for commercial use, the Artist shall be entitled to a minimum of _____ percent of any and all consideration paid or exchanged for such commercial use.

_____   _____

(Artist signature)   Date

_____   _____

(Collector signature)   Date decision. Next are specifics regarding how many changes you'll make in the original design and beyond these, your charge. The last two points are important: They clarify that if the client stops the project at this point, the design returns to you, you retain the design fee, and the design agreement is terminated. If, on the other hand, you are to proceed with the project, then notification is given here that the client must sign an Artwork Commission Agreement and pay you one-third of the final price at the time of signing.

3. If your negotiations have gone well or your design fee is high enough to absorb routine expenses, you might not need this section. But consider including it because it stipulates that the client pays for all expenses connected with producing the design, including shipping, insurance, and delivery charges. You, of course, are responsible for providing the client with an itemized sheet and receipts.

4. This point clarifies that the copyright and all reproduction rights remain with you; the design is your property, not the client's; and your permission is needed if the client wants to publicly display or commercially use the design. If you agree to let the client make a commercial use of your design, you're entitled to royalty on any money made from its use.

Both parties sign the agreement; retain one copy for your files.

Artwork Commission Agreement

Once the design has been approved, you and your client are ready to move to the actual commission agreement (pages 108-109).

The agreement begins with the names and addresses of the two parties involved, the Collector and the Artist, and reiterates that the client has selected a design, given final approval, and wishes to proceed with the work. The work is described.

1. Payment for a commissioned work of art is best broken into three installments; the first three parts of this section detail the due dates and payment amount. If the client wishes only two payments, change the contract accordingly. If the client insists upon only one pay-

ment, change paragraph A to read: "Collector agrees to pay to Artist (amount) upon delivery of the Artwork" and eliminate paragraph B and final payment information in paragraph C. *Never* deliver a completed commission before receiving payment. Further, it states the client must sign a sales agreement and is responsible for paying sales tax.

Paragraph D frees you to follow your judgment in creating the final work while keeping to the style and intent of the design. Some clients object to design changes and desire notification of any problems. In this case, change the last line to read: "If major changes in the design are required, Artist will notify Collector to determine a solution agreeable to both parties."

2. This section states the delivery date and protects you against late delivery. If you cannot complete the commission for any reason, paragraph B protects you. You must return any progress payments, but the design payment, agreed to under a separate contract, remains yours. It also clarifies that the rights to the work, design, and concept remain with you. You might include here a clause specifying that delivery costs are the client's responsibility. This is wise if the client is out of town and if you're not including a provision for expenses. If you included one in your Design Agreement, it's advisable to include one in this contract also.

3. If your contract includes progress payments, this section is necessary to stipulate the consequences if the client is late with a payment. It also states that delay in payment may mean the final delivery date is proportionately extended.

4. This clause notifies the client that he/she can terminate the agreement if dissatisfied, but you keep all payments made (or entitled to) prior to the notification. You can add an escape clause for yourself, especially if you believe this client might be impossible to work with, such as "Artist reserves the right to cancel this contract on ten (10) days' notice." Clarification of returning money is in section 2.

5. This point clarifies that you retain rights and title to the work until final payment is made and the sales agreement signed. Your

sales agreement should spell out that the copyright and all reproduction rights to the work remain with you unless other arrangements have been made.

6. This brief clause covers the eventuality that, if a dispute arises, the aggrieved party is entitled to have his/her attorney's fees paid and to receive any additional available remedy.

Both parties sign the agreement. Retain one copy for your files.

MODEL RELEASE

A written, signed model release is the best way for you to protect yourself from invasion of privacy lawsuits. Most ordinary citizens possess the right of privacy and, because we do, artists who include recognizable people within their paintings must take care not to infringe upon this right.

The right of privacy is recognized in nearly every state, but specific state statutes vary. Although it's your responsibility to find out the exact position and laws of the state you're bound by, some basic information is provided here.

Generally speaking, four categories of privacy invasion exist. Using New York's statutes (upon which many other states' are based), an individual's privacy can be invaded by the use of the person's photograph, likeness, or name for purposes of advertising or trade without consent. If you modify a person's appearance to the point where he/she is no longer recognizable, and no name is associated with the image, then it's unlikely that an invasion of privacy under this category can occur.

But, if any people *are* recognizable, it's advisable to obtain written releases immediately, even if, at this point, you have no intention of using the painting for advertising or trade. You might now be creating a painting for editorial usage in a magazine, in which case a release is probably not necessary, but the painting could eventually wind up for sale in a gallery or be reproduced as an ad; in these cases, releases are definitely advisable. Once a painting is made available for sale to the public, it can be defined as having a *trade* purpose. Without re-

leases, you might have to pass up a potential sale or place yourself in jeopardy of a lawsuit.

The nature of the painting containing recognizable people also dictates the release requirement. People simply in a public place, such as a painting of a street scene, must give consent for you to use their images, that is, sign model releases. But if the people are involved in a public *event*, then they lose some of their right of privacy and releases might not be necessary. Needless to say, this point is open to debate and interpretation.

These are but a few of the factors to be considered when dealing with the issue of privacy. Because of the various interpretations that are possible, differing state laws, and the capricious nature of a painting's future, it's the wise artist who obtains model releases immediately from all recognizable people in the painting. You're saving yourself a lot of possible headaches.

The Model Release presented here (see page 110) is written as a simple contract, is general, and grants broad usage rights to the artist. Essentially, the "model" is giving you, your successors, agents, and legal representatives permission to do whatever you want to with his/her image and/or name. Some models won't agree to such broad usage; in this case, modify the release to state the specific uses the model will allow.

The opening line, "In consideration of $_____, which I have received . . . ," makes this a written contract. For any document to be a binding contract, "consideration" must be given by both parties. The model is giving up something; therefore, you the artist must also give up something, in this case, a certain amount of money. The amount can be as little as one dollar—just so you and the model are exchanging something of value.

A release does not have to be expressed in contract form to be valid. A valid release can be written without the "consideration" line and simply begin with "I, ____(name)____, hereby consent and give ____(artist's name)____, . . ." The drawback to a simple release, however, is that a release can be revoked if a model wishes to take back his or her consent; a contract is more binding.

Artwork Commission Agreement

Artist: Collector:

Name _____   Name _____

Address _____   Address _____

City State Zip _____   City State Zip _____

Phone (_____) _____   Phone (_____) _____

WHEREAS, the Collector has selected the design and given final approval for Artist to proceed with the

creation of this Artwork:

Title: _____

Materials: _____

Approximate completed size: _____

Description: _____

Price: _____

the parties mutually agree as follows:

1. PAYMENTS AND SCHEDULE:

    A. Collector agrees to pay to Artist one-third of the price of the Artwork ($ _____) at this time or
    within ten (10) days.

    B. Collector agrees to pay an additional one-third of the cost of the Artwork ($_____) when the
    Artwork is approximately two-thirds completed. Documentation of the progress of the Artwork may be
    made by photographs of the Artwork or by the personal inspection of the Collector at the discretion of
    the Artist.

    C. Upon nearing completion of the Artwork, the Artist will give the Collector five (5) days advance
    notice of the specific date of delivery so that Collector will be ready to receive the Artwork, make the
    final payment ($_____), and sign a Transfer of Work of Art Agreement or Sale Agreement. Sales
    tax will be paid at this time ($_____).

    D. It is understood and agreed that it may not be possible to recreate the Artwork exactly as depicted
    in the design, and the Artist shall be bound to use his/her best aesthetic judgment to create the Artwork
    according to the style and intent of the design. The Artist is free to make design modifications as the
    Artwork progresses.

2. DELIVERY:

   A. The parties agree that final delivery of the Artwork will be made on or about ____date____. Artist will make every effort to honor and meet this deadline. It is agreed that this date is an estimate only and Artist shall not be responsible for any general, special, or consequential damages for failing to deliver by this estimate date. Artist will immediately notify Collector of any delay occurring or anticipated.

   B. If Artist is unable to finish the Artwork within sixty (60) days of the estimate delivery date, or is unable to produce the Artwork for any reason, the Artist shall be liable for no special, general, or consequential damages, but the Artist shall return all payments received under this Agreement. The Artist shall retain all rights to the concept, design, and the Artwork itself.

3. DELAYED PAYMENTS: In the event Collector fails to make the progress payments when due, interest at the rate of _____ percent per month shall be assessed against the unpaid balance due. In addition, the Artist retains all previous payments plus all rights to the Artwork until full payment is made. It is understood that delay of any payment may proportionately extend the time required to complete the Artwork.

4. TERMINATION OF AGREEMENT: If Collector does not find the Artwork as it progresses fulfilling his/her expectations or needs and therefore wishes to terminate the Agreement, Collector shall immediately notify the Artist of the termination. Artist shall be entitled to retain all payments which Artist has received or was entitled to receive pursuant to this Agreement prior to such notification. Artist shall retain all rights to the concept, design and Artwork, including the right to complete, exhibit and sell the Artwork.

5. TRANSFER OF ARTWORK: It is acknowledged and hereby stated that Artist retains all rights and title to the Artwork until final payment has been received and the Transfer of Work of Art Agreement or Sale Agreement has been duly completed and signed by the parties.

6. ATTORNEY'S FEES: In any proceeding to enforce any part of this agreement, the aggrieved party shall be entitled to reasonable attorney's fees and any available remedy.

_____   _____
(Artist signature)   Date

_____   _____
(Collector Signature)   Date

Model Release

In consideration of $ _____, which I have received, I _____(name)_____ hereby consent and give _____(artist's name)_____, his/her successors, legal representatives, and assigns the right to use my name (or any fictional name), photograph, picture, or portrait in all forms and media, for any and all purposes including publication and advertising of every description, trade, or any other lawful purposes. No claim of any kind will be made by me. No representations have been made to me.

I hereby warrant that I am of legal age and have every right to contract in my own name; that I have read the above authorization and release prior to its execution; and that I am fully familiar with its contents.

Name _____   Date _____

Address _____

City State Zip _____

Witness _____   Date _____

Address _____

City State Zip _____

The model release form you use is an individual decision. Some artists prefer to take their chances with a simple release form because they've discovered that once the money issue is raised, some models request much more than a dollar for the usage the artist is requesting. Others, however, prefer to deal with that negotiation and use the contractual form rather than be concerned about a model revoking consent some time in the future.

If your model is a minor, the release form must be signed by a parent or legal guardian, and it's advisable to have any release witnessed.

For more information about these and other contract situations, refer to North Light's *The Artist's Friendly Legal Guide*, Tad Crawford's *Legal Guide for the Visual Artist*, Toby Klayman's *The Artists' Survival Manual*, and the *Graphic Artists Guild Handbook: Pricing and Ethical Guidelines*. California Lawyers for the Arts, Artist's Equity, and Volunteer Lawyers for the Arts also offer contract information.

COPYRIGHT

Copyright is the federal law that allows creators of original artworks protection from unauthorized copying by others and control over where and how their works' images are used. The law was revised in 1976; the revision became effective January 1, 1978. One of the greatest benefits of this revision is that copyright ownership belongs to you, as the creator of an original work of art, as soon as the artwork is completed or, as the copyright law states, it's set down in a "fixed, tangible medium of expression."

Ownership is automatic; no registration need take place for it to occur. But registering the copyright with the Copyright Office does have its advantages:

- The certificate of copyright helps to prove your copyright claim and the truth of statements made in the application. If an infringement occurs, your copyright must be registered in order to bring a lawsuit against the infringer.
- Your work must be registered *prior* to an infringement (or within three months of

publication, if a published work) to qualify to receive attorney's fees and statutory damages.
- It helps stop some defenses that can be made by an innocent infringer.

Registration is not difficult. To register your work, you need Form VA (Visual Art), the appropriate deposit of materials, and a $10 fee. To obtain the form and a free Copyright Information Kit, write U.S. Copyright Office, Library of Congress, Washington, D.C. 20559. Instructions regarding the specific deposit material appropriate for your artwork are given in the brochures that will be sent to you, but usually, for a one-of-a-kind painting, the Copyright Office requests photographs or slides showing the copyrightable image.

You can register unpublished works as a group for the same $10 fee, and there's no limit to the number of works in the group. For group registration:

- The works must be assembled in an orderly fashion.
- They must bear a single title that identifies the works as a whole, such as "Collected Acrylic Paintings of John Smith, 1989."
- The person claiming copyright in each work must be the same person claiming copyright to the collection as a whole.
- All of the works in the collection must have been done by the same person or the same person has contributed copyrightable work to each work in the collection. Works registered when unpublished do not have to be registered again when publication occurs.

Copyright Notice

To let the public know of your claim to this work's copyright, it's necessary to place a copyright notice on the work in such a manner and location as to "give *reasonable notice*"; that is, anyone looking for the notice can find it after a "reasonable" search. A copyright notice does not *have* to appear on a work until it is published, that is, reproduced in copies. But it's recommended the notice be placed on a work as soon as it's completed to prevent confusion among unknowledgeable clients and avoid accidental publication without notice.

The notice for visual works of art consists of three elements:

- The letter "c" with a circle around it; the word "copyright"; *or* the abbreviation "copr."
- The year date.
- The name of the copyright owner.

A complete notice would read, "© 1986 John Smith." To avoid any dispute regarding the notice's accessibility, it's advised that the copyright notice be placed on the front of two-dimensional works; many artists incorporate it into their signatures. An alternative is to attach the notice to the back of the work or on any backing, mounting, matting, framing, or other material to which the work is durably attached or in which it is permanently housed. If there's concern that the framing or mounting might someday be removed, jeopardizing your notice, write the notice on the back of the actual paper or canvas of the work itself and then place an accessible label on the backing of the work. Because the photographs and slides you use as samples are copies of your works, you should place the copyright notice on the mounts of slides and the backs of photographs with your other labeling.

Reproduction Rights

As owner of a copyright, you also possess intangible exclusive rights to the artwork. For the visual artist, these include the right to:

> Reproduce the copyrighted work in copies;
> prepare derivative works based upon the
> copyrighted work; and, distribute copies . . .
> of the copyrighted work to the public by sale,
> or other transfer of ownership, or by rental,
> lease or lending.

You can sell, give away or keep all portions of these exclusive rights. They're the means by which you profit from the use of the same image repeatedly and maintain control over where and how the work is used. These are the "reproduction rights" that you transfer to clients who want to copy (reproduce) your work.

You can word the rights that you're transfer-

ring as narrowly or as broadly as you wish. For example, if you sell *first rights* to a client, you are transferring the right to first reproduce that work's image; you can't allow it to be used by anyone else until this client has exercised his right to be first. If you narrow it down, however, to perhaps *first limited edition print rights* (assuming this is a print publisher), the client has the right to be first to reproduce the image as a limited edition print, but all other rights are still available and yours to be sold. If the client wants to use it for anything other than a limited edition print, then she must receive your permission and, presumably, pay you for this additional right. If you sell *all rights* to a client, you are giving him total reproduction control of the image. You might own the original work, but clients who buy all rights can reproduce your work where and how they wish; you cannot.

Exclusive rights are those that can be used by only one person at a time, such as first rights (only one person can be "first"). They can only be transferred in writing. *Nonexclusive rights* (those that can be owned by more than one person at a time, such as "one-time rights") can be transferred verbally, though it's a good idea to have the transfer in writing.

The right to use your work's image is completely separate from owning the actual artwork. Therefore, when you sell the original artwork, you retain the copyright and all reproduction rights unless other arrangements have been negotiated. The new owner of the original work cannot copy it without your permission. Likewise, the purchase of one or more rights to the work's image does not give the client the right to keep the original work; artists should always request that original work be returned to them once the client has used the work.

It is your responsibility to keep track of the rights sold on each piece so that exclusive rights are not inadvertently sold to two clients.

Copyright law is filled with subtle interpretations, with some still being tested in the courts. This chapter presents only the basics. It's important that you are aware that you can control where and how your works' images are used and can profit from your creativity.

CHAPTER SIX CHECKLISTS

Being self-employed means:
- [ ] Finding out local business regulations
- [ ] Possible business registration in city or county
- [ ] Adhering to zoning regulations
- [ ] Obtaining a tax identification number (if applicable)
- [ ] Filing sales tax returns with the state (if applicable)
- [ ] Filing state income tax forms (if applicable)
- [ ] Filing Schedule C with federal income tax forms
- [ ] Maintaining accurate records of expenses and income

Standards used by IRS to determine business or hobby status:
- [ ] How an artist conducts business
- [ ] Expertise of artist
- [ ] Time and effort expended by artist on producing artwork
- [ ] Expectation artworks will increase in value
- [ ] Success in prior business activities
- [ ] Artist's history of art income and losses
- [ ] Amount of profits compared to expenses
- [ ] Financial status of artist
- [ ] Elements of personal recreation or pleasure

The long bill of sale:
- [ ] Gives you continuing control over your work
- [ ] States selling price of artwork
- [ ] Gives you notice of exhibition
- [ ] Requires you to give history of artwork
- [ ] Allows you to borrow work for exhibition
- [ ] Prohibits purchaser from changing or damaging artwork
- [ ] Grants you the right to restore work
- [ ] Allows you to share in revenues earned from artwork
- [ ] Clarifies copyright and reproduction right ownership

- [ ] Provides a notice regarding existence of contract for artwork
- [ ] States your moral right to preserve reputation and artwork integrity
- [ ] Continues power of contract beyond death of either party
- [ ] Stipulates payment of legal fees
- [ ] Acknowledges artwork received in perfect condition
- [ ] Should be signed and dated by both parties

An artist/gallery consignment agreement:
- [ ] Confirms gallery receives works in good condition
- [ ] Describes consigned artworks
- [ ] Designates gallery agency is over only described artworks
- [ ] Clarifies copyright and reproduction right ownership
- [ ] Specifies payment period(s) for monies due you
- [ ] Specifies responsibility for care
- [ ] Clarifies removal policy
- [ ] Allows you to borrow works
- [ ] Permits gallery to return works
- [ ] Clarifies contract termination policy
- [ ] Hampers taking of artworks by gallery creditors
- [ ] Should be signed and dated by both parties

Agreements for commissions:
- [ ] Should cover both design and actual creation
- [ ] Allow client to communicate ideas to artist
- [ ] Describe project to be created
- [ ] Permit design fee to be separate from creation fee
- [ ] Specify fee for design
- [ ] Specify creation fee and how to be paid
- [ ] State delivery dates and shipping/ insurance responsibility
- [ ] Clarify copyright and reproduction right ownership
- [ ] Clarify late payment penalty
- [ ] Provide for contract termination
- [ ] Should be signed and dated by both parties

RESOURCES

ORGANIZATIONS

Artists Equity Association, Inc.
PO Box 28068
Central Station
Washington DC 20038

California Lawyers for the Arts
Building C, Room 255
Fort Mason Center
San Francisco CA 94123

Graphic Artists Guild
11 W. 20th Street
New York NY 10011

Society of Illustrators
128 E. 63rd Street
New York NY 10021

Volunteer Lawyers for the Arts
Third Floor
1285 Avenue of the Americas
New York NY 10019

BOOKS

*American Art Galleries: The Illustrated Guide
to Their Art and Artists*
by Les Krantz
Facts on File
460 Park Avenue South
New York NY 10016

The Arthur Young Tax Book
Ballantine Books
201 E. 50th Street
New York NY 10022

The Artist's Friendly Legal Guide
North Light Books
1507 Dana Avenue
Cincinnati OH 45207

An Artist's Handbook on Copyright
Georgia Volunteer Lawyers for the Arts
Plaza Level 16
42 Spring Street Southwest
Atlanta GA 30302

Artist's Market
Writer's Digest Books
1507 Dana Avenue
Cincinnati OH 45207

The Artists' Survival Manual
by Toby Klayman with Cobbett Steinberg
Charles Scribner's Sons, Inc.
866 Third Avenue
New York NY 10022

*The Graphic Artist's Guide to Marketing and
Self-Promotion*
by Sally Prince Davis
North Light Books
1507 Dana Avenue
Cincinnati OH 45207

*The Graphic Artists Guild Handbook: Pricing
and Ethical Guidelines*
Graphic Artists Guild
11 W. 20th Street
New York NY 10011

How to Prepare Your Portfolio
by Ed Marquand
Art Direction Book Company
10 E. 39th Street
New York NY 10016

How to Protect Your Creative Work
by David A. Weinstein
John Wiley & Sons
605 Third Avenue
New York NY 10158

J.K. Lasser's Your Income Tax
Prentice Hall
Prentice Hall Building
Sylvan Avenue
Englewood Cliffs NJ 07632

Legal Guide for the Visual Artist
by Tad Crawford
Madison Square Press, Inc.
10 E. 23rd Street
New York NY 10010

Photographing Your Artwork
by Russell Hart
North Light Books
1507 Dana Avenue
Cincinnati OH 45207

Writer's Market
Writer's Digest Books
1507 Dana Avenue
Cincinnati OH 45207

PERIODICALS

American Artist
1515 Broadway
New York NY 10036

American Indian Art Magazine
7314 E. Osborn Drive, Suite B
Scottsdale AZ 85251

Art Gallery Magazine
Hollycroft Press
Hollycroft
Ivoryton CT 06442

Art in America
Brant Publications
980 Madison Avenue
New York NY 10021

Art Now Gallery Guides
Art Now Inc.
320 Bonnie Burn Road, Box 219
Scotch Plains NJ 07076

Art Now USA
Art Now Inc.
320 Bonnie Burn Road, Box 219
Scotch Plains NJ 07076

Art Today
Web Publications
Box 12830
15100 W. Kellogg
Wichita KS 67235

Art West
303 E. Main Street
Box 1700
Bozeman MT 59715

The Artist's Magazine
F&W Publications
1507 Dana Avenue
Cincinnati OH 45207

ARTnews
5 W. 37th Street
New York NY 10018

The Crafts Report
3632 Ashworth North
Seattle WA 98103

Decor Source Book
Commerce Publishing Co.
408 Olive Street
St. Louis MO 63102

Editor & Publisher
Yearbook
11 W. 19th Street
New York NY 10011

Greetings Magazine
MacKay Publishing Co.
309 Fifth Avenue
New York NY 10016

Modern Photography
ABC Leisure Magazines
825 Seventh Avenue
New York NY 10019

Popular Photography
CBS Magazines
3460 Wilshire Boulevard
Los Angeles CA 90016

Shutterbug
Patch Communications
PO Box F
Titusville FL 32781

Southwest Art
PO Box 460535
Houston TX 77056

Sunshine Artists USA
Sun Country Enterprises Inc.
1700 Sunset Drive
Longwood FL 32750-9697

REFERENCE BOOKS

Encyclopedia of Associations
Gale Research Co.
Book Tower
Detroit MI 48226

Gale Directory of Publications
Gale Research Co.
Book Tower
Detroit MI 48226

Literary Market Place
R.R. Bowker Co.
205 E. 42nd Street
New York NY 10017

Standard Periodical Directory
Oxbridge Communications Inc.
150 Fifth Avenue
New York NY 10011

Thomas Register of American Manufacturers
Thomas Publishing Co.
1 Penn Plaza
New York NY 10017

MATERIALS

CDE Software
948 Tularosa Drive
Los Angeles CA 90026

INDEX

Other Art Books from North Light

Graphics/Business of Art

Airbrushing the Human Form, by Andy Charlesworth $27.95 (cloth)

Artist's Friendly Legal Guide, by Conner, Karlen, Perwin & Spatt $15.95 (paper)

Artist's Market: Where & How to Sell Your Graphic Art, (Annual Directory) $18.95 (cloth)

Basic Graphic Design & Paste-Up, by Jack Warren $13.95 (paper)

Color Harmony: A Guide to Creative Color Combinations, by Hideaki Chijiiwa $15.95 (paper)

Complete Airbrush & Photoretouching Manual, by Peter Owen & John Sutcliffe $23.95 (cloth)

The Complete Guide to Greeting Card Design & Illustration, by Eva Szela $27.95 (cloth)

Creating Dynamic Roughs, by Alan Swann $27.95 (cloth)

Creative Ad Design & Illustration, by Dick Ward $32.95 (cloth)

Creative Director's Sourcebook, by Nick Souter & Stuart Newman $89.00 (cloth)

Design Rendering Techniques, by Dick Powell $29.95 (cloth)

Dynamic Airbrush, by David Miller & James Effler $29.95 (cloth)

Getting It Printed, by Beach, Shepro & Russon $29.50 (paper)

The Graphic Artist's Guide to Marketing & Self Promotion, by Sally Prince Davis $15.95 (paper)

Handbook of Pricing & Ethical Guidelines, 6th edition, by The Graphic Artist's Guild $19.95 (paper)

How to Design Trademarks & Logos, by Murphy & Rowe $24.95 (cloth)

How to Draw & Sell Comic Strips, by Alan McKenzie $18.95 (cloth)

How to Understand & Use Design & Layout, by Alan Swann $24.95 (cloth)

How to Understand & Use Grids, by Alan Swann $27.95

Living by Your Brush Alone, by Edna Wagner Piersol $16.95 (paper)

Marker Rendering Techniques, by Dick Powell & Patricia Monahan $32.95 (cloth)

Papers for Printing, by Mark Beach & Ken Russon $34.50 (paper)

Presentation Techniques for the Graphic Artist, by Jenny Mulherin $24.95 (cloth)

Ready to Use Layouts for Desktop Design, by Chris Prior $27.95 (cloth)

Sir William Russell Flint, by Ralph Lewis and Keith Gardner $55.00 (cloth)

Studio Secrets for the Graphic Artist, by Jack Buchan $29.95 (cloth)

Type: Design, Color, Character & Use, by Michael Beaumont $24.95 (cloth)

Watercolor

Getting Started in Watercolor, by John Blockley $19.95 (paper)

The New Spirit of Watercolor, by MikeWard $27.95 (cloth)

Painting Nature's Details in Watercolor, by Cathy Johnson $24.95 (cloth)

Painting Watercolor Portraits That Glow, by Jan Kunz $27.95 (cloth)

Starting with Watercolor, by Rowland Hilder $24.95 (cloth)

Watercolor Painter's Solution Book, by Angela Gair $24.95 (cloth)

Watercolor—The Creative Experience, by Barbara Nechis $16.95 (paper)

Watercolor Tricks & Techniques, by Cathy Johnson $24.95 (cloth)

Watercolor Workbook, by Bud Biggs & Lois Marshall $19.95 (paper)

Watercolor: You Can Do It!, by Tony Couch $25.95 (cloth)

Mixed Media

Catching Light in Your Paintings, by Charles Sovek $18.95 (paper)

Colored Pencil Drawing Techniques, by Iain Hutton-Jamieson $23.95 (cloth)

The Complete Oil Painting Book, by Wendon Blake $29.95 (cloth)

Exploring Color, by Nita Leland $26.95 (cloth)

Keys to Drawing, by Bert Dodson $21.95 (cloth)

The North Light Illustrated Book of Painting Techniques, by Elizabeth Tate $27.95 (cloth)

Oil Painting: A Direct Approach, by Joyce Pike $26.95 (cloth)

Pastel Painting Techniques, by Guy Roddon $24.95 (cloth)

The Pencil, by Paul Calle $16.95 (paper)

People Painting Scrapbook, by J. Everett Draper $26.95 (cloth)

To order directly from the publisher, include $2.50 postage and handling for one book, 50¢ for each additional book. Allow 30 days for delivery.

North Light Books
1507 Dana Avenue, Cincinnati, Ohio 45207
Credit card orders call TOLL-FREE
1-800-543-4644 (Outside Ohio)
1-800-551-0884 (Ohio only)
Prices subject to change without notice.